PERSONALITY ON THE JOB

Personality on the Job

Kevin Narramore

Servant Publications
Ann Arbor, Michigan

Copyright © 1994 by Kevin Narramore
All rights reserved.

Vine Books is an imprint of Servant Publications
especially designed to serve evangelical Christians.

Published by Servant Publications
P.O. Box 8617
Ann Arbor, Michigan 48107

The names and characterizations in this book drawn from the
author's professional experience are rendered pseudonymously and
as fictional composites. Any similarity between the names and characterizations of these individuals and real people is unintended and
purely coincidental.

Cover design by Steve Eames

94 95 96 97 98   10 9 8 7 6 5 4 3 2 1

Printed in the United States of America

ISBN 0-89283-819-1

Library of Congress Cataloging-in-Publication Data

Narramore, Kevin, 1960-
    Personality on the job / Kevin Narramore.
        p. cm.
    Includes bibliographical references.
    ISBN 0-89283-819-1
    1. Personality and occupation. 2. Typology (Psychology)
3. Interpersonal relations 4. Personnel management.   I. Title.
BF698.9.03N37   1994
158.7—dc20   93-46437

Contents

Special Thanks

I would like to express my appreciation to Jack Dibb, an out-placement consultant, for his thoughts on organizational personality; Jim Pilarski of Marriott for his insights on relating to your boss; Dr. Tom Graham, industrial psychologist, for his generous review of this manuscript; Tom Dorstch of Compass Learning Systems for introducing me to the concept of job-to-person match. Additional thanks to Craig Maloof and Janet Bryson for their support in helping me stay focused; Clark Bowers, for his poetic repertoire; and David Came, for being such a patient and talented editor. To each of you, a heartfelt thanks.

Introduction

Search then, the ruling passion.... this clue, once
found, unravels all the rest.

Alexander Pope, "Essay on Man"

"REPEAT AFTER ME: How happy we would be if Chairman Mao
were alive today."

Disguised as an English lesson, the propaganda messages kept
rolling off the TV screen—and they weren't very subtle. But after
a morning of walking through miles of Shanghai's long winding
seaport, I felt refreshed sitting and watching TV from my hotel
room—even Chinese television. The next "English lesson" phrase
was almost as remarkable as the line about Chairman Mao:
"Repeat after me: I wish I could work twenty-four hours a day...."

I don't know about you, but this ideology differs from my
work ideal. And if you asked those who work the night shift at the
People's Bicycle Factory, I bet they'd like to go home sometime,
too.

In a recent study conducted by Northwestern National Life
Insurance, 1,300 Americans from assembly-line workers to top
management were questioned about the quality of their work life.
The researchers found that 46 percent of the employees reported
feeling highly stressed at work.[1]

"I don't agree with that statistic," reflected Dr. Lewis, a cardi-
ologist friend of mine who is known in our community for being a
caring and dedicated physician. "Why, I love my job. And I think

most people get out of it what they put into it."

"Yes, doctor," I wanted to reply—although I didn't because we were in a patient's room, "I'm sure you love your job. But have you ever stopped to consider that your job and personality are remarkably matched? After all, you're a highly independent person and you get to make your own hours. Match! You're highly analytical and every time you read a medical journal, you're like a kid in a candy store. Match! You have a strong service motive and here you help people almost every day. Match!" For Dr. Lewis, going to work each morning represents energy gain, not energy drain. It's serious fun!

Now let's turn our attention to *you*.

How's the quality of your work life? Does your job leave you under-challenged, mismatched, stressed, or just plain bored? Are you where you'd like to be in your career? Ironically, most people spend more time planning next summer's vacation than they do planning their entire career.

Over the past ten years, I've had the opportunity to interview and survey hundreds of employees about the quality of their work lives, and in many instances, to collect data on their personality profiles. As you might imagine, some people absolutely love their jobs while others come to work every Monday convinced that the week is going to be another disaster. In my experience, whether or not a person finds work to be enjoyable and productive largely depends upon the fit between his or her personality make-up and the "personality" dimensions of the job. These aspects include (a) the work itself, (b) your boss, (c) your co-workers, and (d) the culture or personality of the organization where you hold "citizenship." When these elements are in "sync," work will be enjoyable and fulfilling. When they're not, you're going to psychologically check out of work before you even arrive. Forget about working eight hours a day, let alone the twenty-four hours a day espoused by the communist TV teachers.

Linda, thirty-eight, is a top producing sales representative for a leading midwestern radio station. Her co-workers describe Linda as warm, extroverted, and somewhat assertive as well as quite conscientious, self-disciplined, and service-oriented. These features of Linda's personality contribute to her success.

"I really enjoy the challenge of the sale," Linda says. "I also like meeting people and helping them develop their businesses. Sometimes I'll be driving down the highway, and when I see a business which I think should be advertising with our station, I'll pull over and introduce myself to the owner. Before long, we're great friends and the client signs up for a series of spots. Management keeps wanting to lower my sales commission because I keep exceeding the sales goals. For the most part, I really do like my job. Why should I work somewhere else?"

When asked what she finds most stressful about her work, Linda says, "Sometimes I have such an abundance of paperwork that I feel isolated from people. There are so many documents to prepare and forms to fill out. I wish the station could provide me with a part-time assistant to help handle correspondence, reports, and follow-up letters to new leads. What really gives me heartburn, however, is when something happens to prevent me from keeping my word with a client. I take my commitments very seriously, and it makes me look like such a fool when I promise a client that a spot will be aired on a certain date and the production department doesn't have it ready on time. When this happens, I have to drop everything and drive over to see the client and apologize for what happened."

In Linda's situation, as is true for most people, the two or three most defining personality characteristics that make her so successful—in her case, extroversion, service-orientation, and conscientiousness—can also give her the most grief. Linda loves joining groups, relating to people, and doing the right thing. She dislikes isolation from people and gets ulcers when she can't deliver what she promises.

YOUR "HOT BUTTONS" MAKE A DIFFERENCE

A few years ago I received a call from an executive recruiter who asked about a contact of mine who might make a good didate for a position. One of the first questions that Allen, the recruiter, asked was, "What are two or three of his hot buttons? What really makes him tick?"

Have you ever thought about your own personality "hot buttons"? Although most of us have some insight into why we do what we do, there are many things about ourselves that we don't understand. And even the most insightful person may not apply what he knows about his personality to actual work situations.

If, for example, you have power or control needs, does your job give you opportunities to make significant decisions or to manage others? If you're a "people person," does your job give you opportunities to build enjoyable working relationships with others? If you are highly analytical, does your job give you enough information or challenge? Perhaps you have a difficult boss or co-worker. Have you thought about how to create a win-win partnership based upon how you interact in that difficult work relationship? Are you in the right vocation?

Understanding how your personality affects the quality of your work life is very important because so much time is spent at work. It has been estimated that the average working American spends *forty-two* hours each week on the job. The average professional spends *fifty-two* hours, while the average small business owner spends *fifty-seven* hours each week at work!

Regardless of whether you devote twenty or seventy hours each week on the job, your personality will affect the quality of your work experience; and that, in turn, will influence such things as your earning power, potential for career advancement, quality of relationships on the job, and even your physical health! Considering the tremendous influence that personality has on our lives, the benefits of understanding ourselves and others become enormous.

But how do you gain the necessary insight to effectively change or improve a work situation? First, you must understand more than just the technical skills that are part of your job. You need to delve into the motivational and relational dynamics behind situations. As the great English poet and essayist Alexander Pope wrote, if you "search then, the ruling passion....this clue, once found, unravels all the rest."

HOW TO USE THIS BOOK

This book is divided into two main parts. The first eight chapters deal with personality on the job. They describe major personality patterns in addition to individual subfactors which contribute to your patterns. The major patterns provide a basic understanding of what happens when several personality factors are combined. Individual subfactors are also important because they have a more specific influence on how you and your co-workers tend to think and act. A chapter on the pattern of extroversion, for example, is broken down into the subfactors of exuberance and enthusiasm, risk, sociability, and warmth.

The last four chapters dealing with personality at work apply the various personality patterns and factors to specific work situations such as working with a boss, honing one's communication skills, understanding your organization's personality, and resolving conflicts with co-workers.

Personality: Both Unique and Similar. Have you ever stopped to think that there is no one exactly like you anywhere in the world? I know this sounds like Mr. Rogers, but it's true! Each human being is a mystery known only to God. The individuality of your genetic codes can't be duplicated even if you have an identical twin.

Your personality is unique too. It has been influenced by a complex combination of genetics, parenting, schooling, siblings, friends, spiritual factors, and a host of events and situations. You really can't get to know someone completely in just a few months of living or working together. Nor can you figure everything out about a person simply by giving him a psychological personality test. It takes a lifetime. And even then, more mystery still remains. Just ask a couple celebrating their fiftieth wedding anniversary!

While it is true that you are absolutely unique, it is also true that you have a lot in common with other people. Many psychologists believe that distinct personality styles begin to appear by the time a person is a pre-adolescent and that they tend not to change very radically throughout life. According to psychologist James Dobson, you can often observe the genetic influences on personality when a newborn is placed in the hospital nursery.[2] By the time children are attending school, the effects of home environment and other influences are increasingly visible.

As nurture and nature continue to take their course, adults develop definite patterns of thinking and behaving. In my experience, the more insight you have into your personality and the personality styles of your co-workers, your boss, and others, the more satisfying your job will be.

WHAT IS PERSONALITY?

Throughout history, chroniclers of human nature have been trying to map out human personality traits. Personality, simply defined, is the consistent way a person tends to think and act over a period of time. That's why we talk of personality styles or patterns.

From the days of the early Greeks, philosophers have been working on a system to define personality. During medieval times, the four humors of blood, bile, fire, and phlegm were believed to be responsible for a person's character and temperament. But in 1928 Carl Jung observed that there are four functions by which people operate: feeling, thinking, sensation, and intuition.[3]

In recent years a whole smorgasbord of personality theories and tests have been designed to help us better understand ourselves and others. From the simplest two-factor model, "A or B" sort, all the way up to a thirty-factor model. The complexity of personality allows endless schemes to represent it. What may seem distinct in one system of analysis may blend into another trait or factor in a different system.

In my experience, personality schemes with too few factors are

often overly simplistic, reducing complex human beings to carica-
tures and stereotypes. This approach is only slightly more practical
than asking people if they're a dog or a cat lover, a mayonnaise
connoisseur or a Miracle Whip™ fan. On the other hand, a thirty-
factor model is so complex that even a professional, let alone a lay
person, sometimes has difficulty remembering all the patterns.

In this book, we will identify and develop eight major personality styles, each of which will have its own grouping of subfactors.
Some of the subfactors overlap into more than one pattern. Yet
the different shadings—even if subtle—represent the uniqueness
of the human personality. In my opinion, a more "black-and-
white" approach would be reductionistic.

The personality types I discuss in this book are drawn from the
work of several leading personality psychologists: Dr. Raymond
Cattell, who in 1949 used sophisticated research techniques to
identify sixteen unique personality factors[4]; Drs. Paul Costa and
Robert McCrae whose "Big Five" system[5] theorizes five personality domains and thirty differing personality facets; Dr. Douglas
Jackson and his twenty-one factor Personality Research Form
Instrument;[6] and Thomas Dorstch, creator of the Personal
Preference Inventory and the Job Perception Inventories[7] that
measure individual motivation. From this information, much of
which overlaps, I have synthesized eight major personality patterns
and their supporting subfactors in a way that, based on my consulting experience, have meaning to the work situation.

To protect the identities of the companies and individuals who
have taken part in my research and consulting projects, I have
altered the details of specific cases or combined several companies
or individuals into composites.

A few words of caution are in order here. When focusing on
various personality patterns and especially individual factors, it's
important to remember that each person is a unique combination
of many facets that form a distinct personality. Also, in order to
describe various personality factors, *extremes of a trait are described
for the sake of clarity*. Of the various factors that comprise a person's personality, the average person has only a few extremes. Your

"hot buttons," however, can help explain to a great extent how you think and what you do.

Over-emphasizing one personality factor without understanding how it fits with other "hot buttons" tends to create a misleading or artificial understanding of a person. This is especially true when we notice that some people seem to behave quite differently at work than they do at home.

Brian, thirty-three, is an engineer who works as a manager with a large manufacturing firm. On a psychological test Brian would score about average on the assertiveness scale. At home Brian acts wimpy—he lets his wife tell him what to do. At work, however, he becomes a "dictator"—they call him "The Terminator." If assertiveness was the only filter you used to see Brian, it would be misleading because there are other, more pronounced aspects of his personality that explain the big picture. Why is Brian "Captain Courageous" at work? The answer may lie in two important areas—insecurity and rulekeeping.

Brian is quite insecure and has a troubled sense of self-worth. Work, to Brian, is more than just a way to earn a living for himself and his family. It's an opportunity for self-approval and bolstering his self-esteem. At work Brian is more knowledgeable than others in his functional area. This "expert" status gives him something he wants, but apart from work, never gets. Brian is also very trustworthy and conscientious. He's like a big Boy Scout. This means that he is careful about always following the rules, and when others try to break them, he insists that they conform. Lastly, Brian likes to do his work at a mastery level. His motto is, "If it's worth doing—it's worth doing well." So, when employees for whom Brian is responsible turn out second-rate work, it's an opportunity for him. Not only can he correct them for not producing up to standard, it's also safe for him to be powerful by insisting that standards be met.

Because Brian acts assertively in some areas and nonassertively in others, his true assertiveness style is, as the test indicated, average or flexible. One's most pronounced styles, however, will tend to be consistent across most situations. In Brian's case, these would be insecurity and conscientiousness.

Our understanding, then, of another's personality is only partial because we seldom know what is going on inside of another person. In the final analysis, full knowledge of ourselves and others eludes us and is only known by God, our Creator!

Now let's turn to the first personality pattern. The big question here is, are you a people person or a private person? What about your boss? Your co-workers?

1

The People Person Versus the Private Person

Subfactors for Personality Pattern:
Play, Service, Relatedness, Dependency

BILL AND I USED TO WORK TOGETHER in a nonprofit counseling organization. He was a writer and assistant editor of the company magazine. Beside being a hard worker, Bill had a reputation for being warm and friendly. He spent a lot of time helping people learn how to use the MacIntosh computer. When a system would "crash and burn," Bill would see if he could help. His motives were genuine. Occasionally when visitors arrived, he gave them a tour of the campus. Bill genuinely enjoyed talking with people about his job and the publications department. Bill and other friendly staff members made the organization a very warm and human place to work. This is not untypical of many nonprofit religious organizations which place a high priority on harmonious work relationships.

In contrast, Mark is a physicist with a biotech firm. He is respected for producing outstanding research in his field. A rather solitary and cool person, Mark is not known to be congenial or expressive. He graduated, however, among the top in his class at Massachusetts Institute of Technology. In addition to his being extremely bright, Mark's high collegiate honors were probably due, in part, to the fact that he was indifferent to the people around him. Consequently, he was never sidetracked from his studies by social distractions such as parties and football games. Mark relates primarily to ideas and theories rather than human beings. He is a task-oriented doer.

Bill and Mark represent opposites in terms of people orientation. While most people fit more into the middle of this continuum, it is helpful to understand the type with which you can most identify and why.

ARE YOU A PEOPLE PERSON OR A PRIVATE PERSON?

How do you recognize a people person? Is he or she an extrovert who joins groups and tells great jokes at parties? Sometimes, but not necessarily. Not all extroverts are eager to relate closely to those around them. A people person may also be the guy who goes to a party hoping that a close friend will show up and spend the evening talking with him. If you're a "people person" like Bill, you will find great enjoyment relating closely to others. Your friendly, cooperative, and supportive style will make you popular because others will see you as approachable, hospitable, and fun. *In a real sense you are meeting a need in their lives.*

People persons are generally warmhearted and easygoing. They are emotionally open and socially congenial. They often find satisfaction in relational occupations where social opportunity and service is involved, such as selling, social work, religious work, counseling, consulting, human resources, and many medical jobs.

Private persons tend to be formal, reserved, detached, and idea-oriented. If you fit this description, you will probably excel in a career that allows you to work alone and in a job that calls for precision and dealing with abstract ideas and theories. You'll be more like Mark than Bill. Jobs of an editorial nature, research, and certain types of art are often good fits. Those types of occupations will allow you to relate more closely with the work itself rather than with other people. Organizationally, you may tend to excel in businesses that are also more task-oriented. In California there is a large utility company, for example, where all the executive offices are spacious and walled off from each other. Secretaries serve as the gatekeepers. Social contacts between the various offices are limited; the communication style is formal and task-oriented.

Down the street is another energy company where the executive offices have glass panels adjacent to the doors, which allows others to look in and see what's going on. Most everybody leaves his or her door open, and the conference rooms have frosted glass partitions rather than plaster walls or wood panels. The implicit sense of mission is noticeably more social. The architecture and office arrangements suggest open communication and availability.

In American culture, those who are not people persons are often regarded by other employees as unfriendly, distant, cold, or inflexible. Bosses usually give private persons fewer promotions than those with high interpersonal preferences. The irony is that although private persons may be thought of as nonsocial, and therefore are passed over for that reason, very often they are some of the most productive doers in a company. When they find their niche, they can really produce. Are private persons unhappy because they don't relate easily to other people? Not necessarily. Often they relate more to things and ideas, rather than to other human beings.

HIGH PLAYERS

Fun lovers are known to be people persons who are high on the "play factor." They tend to be lighthearted, and want their work to be—you guessed it—fun. High players approach work as a way to have a good time and respond well to other lighthearted co-workers. Their strength lies in positive personal relationships and finding enjoyment in almost anything. They enjoy making people feel good about their experiences with them. As you can imagine, they dislike "wet blankets."

Co-workers who have high play preferences are sometimes misunderstood as being "goof-offs" who waste time on frivolities. If you're a supervisor or a boss, you should avoid evaluating Mr. or Ms. Fun on anything other than his or her actual productivity. If you assess these people on the basis of charm or levity, you may overrate them. If you resent them for having too much fun, you may underrate them.

As a manager, it's also important to know what type of assignments are best for high play employees. Bear in mind that when high play employees are doing something that's miserable for them, somebody is bound to pay for it! If an upbeat person is performing a task that he or she enjoys, however, that person is not as likely to ask for a raise or more benefits because the work itself is seen as rewarding. What high players need from you are personal freedom and a clear and consistent understanding of your expectations or limits. Outline the results you expect. At the same time, give them the freedom to have fun as long as they are doing a good job, and they do not interfere with the work progress of others.

Take Greg, the new boss. Everyone was wondering what he would be like. During his first week, Greg called the entire staff together for a meeting. "Regardless of what the current management craze is," said Greg, "I don't believe in the open door policy. By next week, I'll have a light outside my door. When the light is on, do not come in. When the light is off, you may come in at any time whether or not the door is open or closed."

This was in contrast to the previous boss who had a so-called "open door" policy. However, if you walked in at the wrong time, you knew you were unwelcome, and that you probably had blown it.

People persons with high play preferences do well in organizations that convey the following messages: "Here are the boundaries and what we expect you to produce. Are we going to watch over you every minute to check on what you're doing? No. You're responsible adults! Within those limits, we have no objection against your having fun."

The high play person thinks, "If I don't have fun, I'm out of here. Nothing has to be that serious!"

Tips for High Players

- If you're fun-loving, that's okay; just know when to be serious. The biblical model found in Ecclesiastes 3:1 and 4 tells us, "There is a right time for everything:... a time to laugh" and times when we ought to be "somber and reserved." Successful high players have a keen sense of timing. When is it appropriate to do something? Be mindful that your tendency toward playfulness could lead your managers or co-workers to think of you as always goofing off. This is particularly true if your co-workers aren't having as much fun as you are. If this is the case, they'll resent you.

- Be sensitive about the appropriateness of your humor. If, for example, your boss has just been hit with the loss of a large account, it's not the time for a jovial attitude or wisecracks. No matter how "cute" your remarks may be, if the timing is wrong, keep quiet.
- Lighthearted people often try to keep things cheerful by avoiding serious discussions on unpleasant subjects. However, keeping things "light" tends to limit communication to a superficial level so that dealing with more important issues may be postponed. Know when to be serious.
- Remember that work is not always fun and games. If you want a high standard of living, for example, there are tradeoffs. You may have to work hard at things that are not especially enjoyable in order to get ahead and achieve your goal. On the other hand, finding work that's fun may mean less money. You may need to drive an older car and eat at fast food restaurants when you go out for dinner.
- *Managers:* If you're high on playfulness, be careful not to hire or promote people just because you find them to be fun. Just because a person is a fun-lover doesn't necessarily equip him or her with the ability or commitment to do a job well.
- *Managers:* If you're the serious type, don't be a killjoy. Make a point to create an atmosphere that allows for humor and celebration along with your work. Remember the old adage, "All work and no play make Jack a dull boy." Personalities differ, and so must our approaches!

LOW PLAYERS

Those low on the play scale are often doers who equate being serious on the job as part of the work ethic. "Work should be serious.

ous. If you're having fun, something's wrong! After all, 'if you don't work, you shouldn't eat.'" If you are a somber, more task-oriented person, you probably consider a fun atmosphere in the workplace to be a waste of time. Some people will admire your dedication and self-denial. Others may view you as dull and uninteresting. Your life will be very focused on obligations and work, leaving little or no time for fun or impromptu activities.

Doug, for example, is most always serious. He was raised in a "struggling" family. Life was hard. And today, as an adult, he is driven and intense about almost everything, especially his work.

Then there is Bruce, a human resource consultant. His wife, Darla, had formerly been the executive vice president of a mutual fund firm. Eventually she joined her husband in his consulting business. Before working with him, however, Darla felt a measure of resentment. Because Bruce brought such a relaxed, positive attitude to his work, he seemed to be having fun doing it. This caused Darla to think that Bruce wasn't really working. "You can't have all that fun and get anything accomplished" was one of her negative thoughts. But when Darla started working with Bruce in the business, she discovered how diligent he really was. She began to understand that because of his relaxed, upbeat style, he was able to minimize the stress level by setting a positive, fun tone at work.

Tips for Low Players

- As an employee, don't allow yourself to be priggish when others are playful. Many lighthearted people can be very productive while still seeing the humorous side of a situation. Avoid coming across as heavyhanded on issues that are not serious. A little lightheartedness makes the hours pass faster. Try to cultivate more of a sense of humor. It can brighten the day for all of you.

- When working as a member of a team, make a point to be positive. If you're the subdued type, remember that work-group morale can plummet if too many people are unexpressive and grim.

- *Managers:* Be aware of the potentially volatile mix in pairing high players with low players. Because high and low players often

form negative value judgements about each other, you may
need to help them learn how to communicate nondefensively.

- *Managers:* When it is earned, give due recognition to low players
as well as high players. Let both know they are valuable. Since
part of your job is to give employees feedback and provide an
atmosphere that produces rewarding performance, remember
to tailor your communication to employees in a way that will
account for their differences in expressing playfulness. Give the
more sober employees the genuine affirmation they need for
their good work. To the lighthearted, however, your smile combined with an upbeat remark will mean a great deal.

HIGH RELATERS

"I'm going to disconnect your phone. Then we'll see what you
do!" said Dwain, the manager.

"But there are calls I need to return that can be done during the
day. And I'm getting my work done," insisted Mark as he turned
away from his computer with the telephone in one ear.

"Yeah, but you'd get twice as much accomplished if your phone
was disconnected. I've been watching and you've been on the
phone three or four times during the past hour. You're here to
work, pal, and if you don't, I'm going to get someone else who
will produce!"

This is a conversation that I overheard recently in an office. It
took place between a high relater and a low relater who were slug-
ging it out, so to speak, to the point where both their faces were
bright red. Have you heard this same script enacted at your workplace? When one who is a high relater is denied insufficient people
contact, that person will have problems producing, and then management will get all over his or her case.

Do you *thoroughly* enjoy talking with others? Do you find it
emotionally stimulating to converse with the people you meet? Do
you have a reputation for being warm and companionable? Are
you slow to criticize others? Do you find it easy to smile and take a

personal interest in people? Are close relationships among your highest priorities? If so, you're high on the relatedness factor. You're a people person who places a high value on relationships.

You are a warmhearted person who is very interested in forming close, emotional ties with people. You tend to be affectionate, tenderhearted, and sympathetic to the needs and concerns of others.

People who are high relaters often like to spend time listening to and understanding other people's experiences and feelings. They also frequently like to talk and share their own experiences and feelings. However, not every high relater wants to both listen and talk. Rather, some relaters are quiet and just want to listen. They may be more eager to hear about and understand the other person. In any case, high relaters like to be with others and spend time with them in a relaxed setting that isn't focused on completing tasks.

If you and your boss are high relaters, the two of you may get along just fine. Make sure, however, that you're in tune with your boss' expectations for the tasks that he or she wants you to accomplish. In the comraderie that you've developed, your boss' work expectations could easily get lost. If you're a high relater and your boss is not, you may feel that the boss does not care about you personally because he or she doesn't seem to want to hear what you'd like to say, and just wants you to get busy. If there are extreme differences in your relating styles, you may even feel put down or verbally abused. In these situations, employees often blame themselves and wonder, "What am I doing wrong?" If such is the case, you need to understand that you're not the problem—you're just not getting enough positive input and affirmation from your boss.

In terms of organizational fit, I've noticed that high relaters often do well as the gatekeepers of large organizations. Receptionists and secretaries, for example, often have more opportunities to relate with people than do mid-level managers. By virtue of their size, larger organizations often allow employees more opportunities to socialize since with so many hands on deck, employees are less apt to be put under the microscope. In a sense, large organizations give employees an opportunity to "hide out."

On the other end of the organizational chart, a high-relational style is often helpful to top executives who spend considerable time encouraging their staff and developing new contacts. Consider former President Reagan, for example, who developed close relationships with various leaders and spent much of his time networking and building trust rather than micro-managing every detail. His interpersonal skills were more important to him than his technical knowledge of the issues.

When high relaters lose their jobs or retire, they often experience acute depression within a short time of leaving. This is because they had access to so many people contacts at work which they no longer have. It is important, then, for high relaters to develop a network of relationships which extend beyond the workplace.

Tips for High Relaters

- Look for a job that allows you to get to know your fellow workers. Sitting at a computer all day, for example, can leave you feeling isolated and physically drained. The right job for you is one which provides contact with people.
- Guard against allowing your warmhearted nature to prevent you from making tough-minded decisions. Sometimes you have to assume the role of a "bad guy." Force yourself to be objective and firm when dealing with business problems. Ask yourself, is this practical?
- Too many distractions can waste valuable time. Although you may love those interruptions, you may need to close your door or move to a more secluded place every now and then in order to finish your work. Arranging for time to work by yourself every day can free you from the slowdown of interruptions.
- If your co-workers are low relaters, they will respond better to less emotion. Remember not to give too many "warm fuzzies" if they are not appreciated. Co-workers may feel uncomfortable, or even question your sincerity.
- *Managers:* If you are a high relater, be careful about getting too

emotionally involved with your subordinates. A leadership role requires that you make objective employee evaluations. If your feelings get overly-involved, you may hand out halos to people you like, but horns to those who rub you the wrong way.

- *Managers:* If you supervise a high relater, remember that he or she may need considerable personal encouragement. Also, make it a point to spend enough time listening to a high relater. The employee needs to feel that you understand and empathize with his or her work situation.

LOW RELATERS

Do people think of you as somewhat cold or aloof? Do you have few emotional attachments with co-workers? Does standing around and "chatting" with people for an extended period of time bore you or make you feel uncomfortable? If so, you're a low relater.

Low relaters are typically private people who find their greatest satisfaction from personal projects rather than socializing. In fact, they often feel more comfortable being alone, preferring solitude to group activities. If you are a low relater, for example, you're less willing to "donate" your time to others just for the sake of talking. If a high relater exceeds the chit-chat limit, a low relater will want to either cut off the conversation or bring the other person back to the topic since he or she feels that the conversation is not productive. Low relaters will also give nonverbal cues, such as continuing to work on a task or even beginning to move away while the person is still talking.

If your co-worker is a high relater and you're not, you may tend to dislike that person for coming around and wasting your time with unimportant details or personal matters. If your boss is a high relater and you're not, you'll probably feel annoyed during those occasions when you must sit and listen to things that don't interest you and that you don't want to hear. Your boss may view you as unfriendly and distant.

If you're the boss and a low relater, be careful. You may be offending your employees without even knowing it. I remember a bright, middle-aged general manager named Lee, who was the number two man in a certain advertising agency. Lee had a nice blend of concern for people and production. He worked effectively with his staff. By comparison Lee's boss, Dan, who owned the business, was unusually low on most of the interpersonal dimensions—play, relatedness, service, and dependency. Most of Dan's staff viewed him as a cross between a Vulcan and a Klingon. He was almost brutal to be around.

"I'm the buffer, the communication link, between Dan and the other employees," said Lee. This meant that Lee took Dan's cold pricklies, converted them into warm fuzzies, and then gave direction to the staff. Put simply, Lee was the human face of management at the company. The only problem with this arrangement, however, is that Lee could not escape working with Dan.

Dan was so mercilessly task-oriented that Lee was starving for positive feedback. "If Dan made even the slightest positive comment about my work, I would have to multiply it times one thousand," said Lee. Dan, on the other hand, felt that he was just doing his job and didn't see why his staff were such complainers. Each night Lee went home with his stomach tied in knots. After two years of what Lee called "abuse," he resigned.

Low relaters often feel comfortable in fast moving, technical organizations. In these environments you come to work, do your job, and then go home. The socializing? It comes during the annual Christmas party!

Small businesses that deal with moving a product, such as in manufacturing for example, often tend to employ low relaters. With fewer hands on deck, there is often less time for employees to socialize. Another place where you'll tend to find low relaters is in upper mid-managment levels within large organizations. The level just before the top management often has people who are extremely task-oriented. In these environments, a high relater would most often stand out as an oddball.

Tips for Low Relators
• You can do your best work in positions which offer limited social contact. You may prefer solitary pursuits over group efforts. Too

many people contacts can stress or distract you.

- Co-workers who are high relaters are apt to view you as cold and indifferent. So when you have occasion to meet with business associates, make a point to be sociable. Smile when you enter the room, establish eye contact, ask people about themselves, compliment people and call them by name. Making others feel accepted is an important ingredient of success.

- *Managers:* Remember that a low relater, even though he or she may appear distant and uninvolved, can be an exceptionally productive member of your staff. Make sure, however, that person is allotted sufficient time alone to get his or her job done. Too many meetings may affect a low relator's productivity.

- *Managers:* It is vitally important that you listen to and encourage your employees. Make it a point to compliment each staff member about something at least once every day. This will not only encourage your staff but also make you more approachable in situations where employees need to confer with you about a problem or ask you a question.

HIGH SERVERS

Do you often go the extra mile to help other people? Do you have a reputation for being thoughtful and considerate? Do you frequently consider the other person's best interest? Do you tend to reach out to others?

If so, you're high on the service factor. You're a tender-hearted person with a strong sense of compassion. You're inclined to be sympathetic to a wide range of people.

High servers enjoy work that provides opportunities to reach out and help others. They often do well in altruistic jobs that enable them to nurture the needs of others. Examples are school counselors, human resource personnel, or religious workers. Their greatest satisfaction comes from knowing that others will benefit from their efforts. Often, high servers are well suited to working in Christian or nonprofit organizations that share their same vision and goals.

Not all altruistic professions, however, provide opportunities for service. Many social workers, for example, go into a field with the expectation of helping the less fortunate, only to realize that their job is more about forcing people to get off welfare. Social workers and teachers, for example, who are high servers can be some of the most frustrated and stressed-out people around. This is also frequently true for high servers who join large, urban police departments. They start out with an idealistic mindset, but it doesn't take long before they become very cynical about our justice system and people in general.

If your co-worker places less value on service than you do, you may consider him or her to be pragmatic or cold and heartless. But if your co-worker places more value on service than you do, you may think of him or her either as a nice person or as somewhat naive.

A salesman who is a high server may do very well if he genuinely believes in the product. He may, however, have a difficult time closing a sale if he doesn't feel that it is in the customer's best interest. In that case, he might talk a prospective customer out of a product!

Tips for High Servers

- A job which forces you to be an authoritarian and does not provide you with sufficient opportunities for serving the needs of others may be stressful to you. You'll be happier doing work that coincides with your values of consideration and service to others.
- Don't let your compassionate nature prevent you from making objective decisions. Face it, it's difficult for you not to be biased! Learn to approach business problems from a more detached, objective viewpoint. Consider taking a course in decision-making.
- Beware of the way in which you display your feelings of compassion. Others may take advantage of you and conclude that you are an easy mark or that you can be pushed around.
- Be careful not to invest all your time with co-workers who are the underdogs. The astute worker has a variety of friends and contacts in various levels of the organization.
- *Managers:* If you tend to be a soft touch, remember that a good

supervisor does not allow empathy and personal feelings to interfere with his or her better judgment. Sometimes your job involves making tough choices. List the pros and cons. Be aware of your emotional dynamics. Be objective in your evaluations of organizational needs and employee performance.

• *Managers:* if you have an employee who is high service, try to stress the significance of what he or she does. High service employees want to identify with their work from the standpoint of the good they do in helping others and in making a vital contribution to the organization. Creating a cause makes a high service employee psychologically self-employed.

LOW SERVERS

Do your co-workers see you as selfish, cold, or calculating? Do you get upset with people who complain about problems? Are you choosy about whom you help and in what way? If so, you belong in the category of those who are lower in the service dimension.

This does not mean that as a low server you are unwilling to assist others who are in need of help. Low servers, however, are much more selective in whom they assist and under what conditions. Their involvement with others is seldom the result of a random emotional response. Instead, low servers tend to think things through, thus making rational decisions and deferring to cold, hard logic. Accordingly, they are often good at jobs which call for toughness and critical decision-making skills.

If you're low on service and your co-worker or boss is high on this dimension, you may find the person to be exasperating because his or her decisions seem "unrealistic," too "soft hearted," or "lacking in business savvy." My great-grandfather, Dr. John Nelson Roe, was a physician in Brooklyn, New York. The quintessential high-service type, he would never refuse a needy street person who asked for money. His wife, who was lower on service, objected because she said they were only using it for booze. Their teenage son agreed that it was a rip-off. One particular day, after

Dr. Roe had handed out money to a man with a hard luck story about being hungry, Paul followed the street person just to see what he really did with the money. As expected, the street person headed to the nearest saloon and promptly ordered some whiskey.

"Don't you dare!" ordered Paul, walking up to the bar. "My father didn't give you money to buy booze and you know it! You said you needed money to buy food."

"Hey! Hey!" responded the saloonkeeper after Paul's explanation, "we'll have none of the likes of your kind." And Paul and the saloon keeper together threw the scoundrel out. Low servers tend to be very good at administering "tough love."

Tips for Low Servers

- Consider working in fields that deal in facts or that capitalize on your ability to make no-nonsense decisions. Computer science, physical science, engineering, law enforcement, or middle management in a task-oriented organization are typical examples of good career fits.

- You may lack empathy or understanding into the subtleties of people's problems. When faced with other people's personal needs, try not to make them feel guilty for being "self-indulgent." Your tolerance will go a long way in creating better work relationships with your co-workers or subordinates.

- *Managers:* In supervising low servers, you will be frustrated with their performance if their job calls for them to go out of their way to be helpful to people. If they absolutely must perform high service tasks, communicate clearly your service expectations and the rewards they will receive depending upon how well they do. Monitor their performance carefully.

HIGH DEPENDERS

Is it hard for you to make up your mind? Do you feel apprehensive when left to do a job on your own? *Are you more secure when someone is available who can confirm that you are on the right track?*

Do you often feel like you need someone else to help you in solving a problem? If you are a high depender, you will frequently seek the compassion, affection, counsel, time, or comfort of other people. Without the help and protection of others, you will feel insecure and experience a lot of discomfort.

A line in a recent popular song says, "You know I need relating, not solitude." If everyone sang at work, this is the tune that high dependers would vocalize throughout the day. High dependers don't want to be alone. They are usually unhappy working at jobs where they are isolated from others such as that of a bookkeeper, physicist, or data entry operator.

Why do high dependers seek companionship? Their motives can be quite varied. Some need others around them so that they can exert control. Others need the company of others as a reminder that they have not been abandoned. Psychologists call this *separation anxiety*. High dependers may also have been raised in a family situation where they were over-indulged and over-protected. In addition, some high dependers may be contending with a troubled self-image and may be seeking reassurance from a stronger person for confirmation and advice.

For these reasons, high dependers can be extremely demanding in their work relationships in that they require time and attention from co-workers in order to gratify their own needs. Fellow employees may find them too "sticky." Gaining too much input from others may also be a way of avoiding responsibility. As one high depender confided, "I never realized how clingy I was until one of my co-workers stopped returning my phone calls and pointedly asked me whether or not I had very many friends. I guess I was looking for comfort from the people I worked with at the office."

If you're a boss and your employee has a dependency need, he or she may not discuss disagreements or problems with you directly because your disapproval might result in interpersonal rejection. The employee may, therefore, be rather indirect or non-assertive, which may cause problems, especially in a task-oriented organization where people need to speak and make decisions in a frank and direct fashion.

Tips for High Dependers

- Dependent persons often prefer work situations where there is considerable job security and structure. If you're a high depender, you may also find yourself asking the boss a lot of questions about what is expected of you. If your boss is a busy person, don't bug him or her about every little thing. Write down your questions and wait until you have several items to discuss before paying a visit.

- You operate best when you have a confidant to give you advice or counsel. Finding a mentor may be an invaluable help to your career as well as a way to reduce anxiety. However, be careful not to lean too heavily on a mentor for support or favors. Your dependency can backfire if you overdo it. A person may be happy to help you—but he or she will resent it if you become a pest.

- When problems turn up, avoid going to your co-workers for help unless it's really important. Asking your co-workers or business contacts for favors can make them weary of you. In some instances, it can put them in a difficult position. Guard against being seen as a chronic needer.

- Your need for social support means that you may make decisions based upon what you think others want to hear. As long as you show respect, most people prefer honesty over political correctness. If you are reticent about being direct, consider taking a course on assertiveness training. Individual therapy may also be helpful in getting at the root causes of your overdependency on others.

- *Managers*: With high dependers, make sure you give them enough direction and structure in the workplace. It might be helpful to set aside a couple of minutes every day for meeting with a low depender, so you can address any concerns or issues the person might have.

- *Managers:* If you are a high depender, make sure that you don't smother your employees with too many unnecessary visits or conversations. Because you're the boss, they're less likely to tell you that they don't appreciate your invasion of their "space." Although employees like to be consulted about decisions which affect their work, they also resent it when you lean too heavily on them instead of doing your job as a manager.

LOW DEPENDERS

Are you independent and resourceful? Do you prefer making your own decisions? Do you like working alone? If so, you're probably a private person and you don't rely too heavily on others for reassurance and advice. Rather than depending on others, you customarily face challenges by yourself. Arctic explorers and successful entrepreneurs, for example, are generally more apt to be low dependers than most social workers and hospital volunteers.

Low dependers are not natural joiners of organizations. Instead, they prefer going it alone as an individual. If you're a low depender, you'll rely more on yourself than others. You'll also place great value in your own thoughts. You are most likely not very socially active unless it's in a leadership capacity. Others may conclude that you are not interested in their help or ideas. People probably see you as a "loner" or an individualist.

Tips for Low Dependers
- If you prefer to work alone and make decisions by yourself, your co-workers will peg you as a soloist, rather than a team player. To counteract such personal distancing, make it a point to spend some time with your co-workers and boss. Let others know that you are interested in them personally.
- Your counterparts, who are high dependers, will need you to set some boundaries for them. Otherwise, they are likely to cramp your style.
- *Managers:* If you are a low depender, let your employees know that they are needed and appreciated. Because you are self-sufficient, you may not communicate the importance and significance of their contribution. They need to feel that you are genuinely interested in them. Make sure to compliment and thank employees when they have completed tasks. Be attentive to their needs and moods.

• *Managers:* If you are a low depender, deep inside, you may tend to discredit the ideas and opinions of other people. This means that you must make an effort to listen to others and to accept good advice. Utilizing other people's strengths will be to your ultimate benefit.

SUMMARY

Are you primarily a *people person* or a *private person?* Odds are that if you're a people person, you're more likely to be a "high player," "high relater," "high server," or "high depender." On the flip side of the coin, if you're a private person, you may well be a "low player," "low relater," "low server," or "low depender." Knowing your general preference in relating to others, especially as applied to your individual variations, can be a valuable source of information and insight into yourself, your co-workers, and your career.

As we progress through the next seven chapters on the various personality patterns, keep in mind that there are positive aspects as well as negative ones to most every style. Once you gain insight into the "hot buttons" of your own personality, you can celebrate your preferences and avoid those situations that might put you at a disadvantage on the job. You'll also see why it's often easier to change the job than the person.

The following chapter on extroversion and introversion also focuses on people. The extrovert, however, may not necessarily be a true "people person." You'll find out what this means. After all, it's all in a day's work and a day's relating!

2

Are You an Extrovert or an Introvert?

Subfactors for Personality Pattern: Enthusiasm, Risk, Social Participation.

HAVE YOU EVER THOUGHT about which types of activities give you the most energy? Or, on the other hand, what situations make you feel drained? When you're working by yourself, for example, do you enjoy interruptions such as a phone call or an impromptu visit by a co-worker? At home, do you like to take walks alone and stay up late at night by yourself, or is being by yourself a punishment? At work, do you play it safe or are you a risk-taker? At social gatherings do you entertain your friends by "hamming it up," or are you more quiet and serious?

Introversion and extroversion are general terms commonly used to describe whether people tend to be energized from within or from without. Extroverts come to work with social expectations and enjoy frequent distractions such as phone calls or people stopping by to talk. In fact, work without people usually drains the extrovert of energy. "When I'm with other people," says one extrovert, "I forget about my own problems because I see so many other possibilities when I'm talking with other people present."

At parties, extroverts spend their time networking with others and enjoy meeting a variety of people. Expressive and sometimes even "show offs" or "clowns," extreme extroverts tend to speak first and edit their thoughts later. At least one extrovert should be invited to every party if you want to "cut loose and have fun." Extroverts also tend to enjoy variety, action, and taking risks.

Carol was an executive with a financial firm. Although she was more task- than people-oriented, her employees liked her because she was fair and took good care of them. As Carol's staff increased, the office configuration had to be rearranged; and it was necessary to find a new workspace for her secretary, Kelly, a very sociable young lady. Because of Carol's influence in the organization, she was able to find Kelly a private office. Much to Carol's amazement, Kelly did not seem very excited about moving into a private office and kept inquiring about other possible workspaces. "The only other place would be a small desk down the hall right by the water fountain where everybody goes when they want to stretch and get a drink," said Carol. "I'm sure you wouldn't want that."

Kelly's thoughts, however, were just the opposite. "The more people that can pass by my desk, the better I like it!"

After discussing things further, Carol and Kelly came to an arrangement—Kelly could have the desk everyone walks by as long as she does her work on time. "But if you don't get your work done," said Carol, "I'll have to move you into a private office."

In general, our society has a bias toward extroverts like Kelly. At work, for example, their outgoing, friendly nature makes them more visible to management. Studies show that extroverts receive more promotions than introverts. "She has lots of personality" is considered to be a compliment, while the introvert's personality is considered by some to be less than desirable. People who are not extroverts are often misunderstood and considered low-key, cold, and less friendly.

Are extroverts really "people persons"? Yes and no. On the surface the answer is definitely *yes*. Extroverts gain energy from social contact and often enjoy lively exchanges. Their enthusiasm is contagious. For this reason, they may appear to be very warm and companionable. Their friendliness, however, is not *necessarily* rooted in a deep desire to form close and caring relationships with other people. While some extroverts are genuine people persons, others could care less about other people—even though they may seem quite friendly.

Introverts, on the other hand, may not seem very friendly because of their social inhibitions but may, nevertheless, establish very close and loyal friendships with a few key people. Ron, for example, is an accountant who for the most part is rather shy. He speaks in a soft, yet sincere voice and is completely unassuming. Others hardly know it when he enters or leaves a room. His job involves keeping on top of the finances and he rather enjoys the interpersonal isolation of "crunching" numbers throughout the day. Although Ron is quiet and reserved, if you become ill, he is the first one to send you a card or drop by to see if you need anything—and he means it.

Introverts prefer quiet reflection to discussion. At a party, an introvert will find people contact to be an energy drain. To restore balance after too much people contact, introverts will often start to do a nonsocial task such as cooking or cleaning up. They're quintessential doers. Although introversion is influenced to a certain extent by ethnic and cultural traditions, withdrawing from people too much is unhealthy and the severely introverted would greatly enhance their lives by seeking professional help.

So, generally speaking, extroverts gain energy from social interaction and expression, while introverts find it more energizing to work alone in an atmosphere of reflection. Beyond the broad brush strokes of "extroversion" or "introversion," however, a person's social preferences can be best understood by examining the individual subfactors of this pattern. These include what I will call the "two E's," enthusiasm and exuberance, as well as risk and sociability.

THE TWO "E'S"

If you tend to be colorful, lively, expressive, and like being the center of attention, congratulations! You would probably score high on a psychological test measuring factors such as enthusiasm and exhibitionism. If you're more subdued and emotionally flat, you're probably low on enthusiasm and expressiveness.

"Jay is one big nerve ending," say his co-workers, "he doesn't know when to keep his mouth shut." Besides saying the first thing that comes into his mind, Jay also tends to be impulsive in his actions. While driving home from work one evening, he made an impromptu stop at an office supply store. With no list in hand, he purchased one hundred and twenty-five dollars worth of office products, only to find the next morning that several of the items he had purchased were available free of charge in the company stock room.

Jay's co-worker, Karen, is the opposite. In every meeting she measures her words very carefully. When Karen goes shopping, she never ventures into a store without a list.

High Enthusiasm and Exhibitionism. *La belle de la joue*—the belle of the ball! If you like being the center of attention and tend to be flashy, conspicuous, or dramatic and if you're witty and noticeably clever, then face it, you're a bit of an *exhibitionist*. Your actions are saying, "Hey, everybody, notice me!"

Sean's world centered around himself. If he didn't have everyone's attention, he worked hard at devising ways of getting it. While most people would drink coffee and relax during an office break, Sean was turbocharged and seemed almost hyperactive. Those fifteen-minute breaks turned into a theatrical production where he was the central character of a play and everyone else was a captive audience. When Sean would ask you a question about yourself, it was always a means (and not always so clever) of turning the conversation and the limelight back to *himself*.

Sean is probably not aware of the adverse reactions that he elicits from his co-workers. The truth is that few of us stop to realize how our own communication styles are affecting others—especially if we're sidetracked by our own emotional needs. It's altogether possible that Sean was raised in an environment where he was either overindulged as a child or others did not take the time to listen to him. Unlike Sean, there are some exhibitionists who find careers that fit well with their need for attention.

In the performing and creative arts, in certain forms of academia, and in many sales professions, for example, this personality style can sometimes be an asset. In the best case scenario, one's co-workers may view this colorful and upbeat style as being positive and entertaining. In the extreme, however, it can become tiresome and judged as just too intense.

Tips for High Exhibitionists and Enthusiasts

- While certain high profile jobs fit well with people who like to be expressive and visible, remember that being a star at the expense of your work group can cause others to think of you as immature, or worse, egocentric. So before taking center stage, ask yourself if what you want to say is really necessary or whether you would be monopolizing the conversation. Being a skillful listener will go far in gaining the respect and admiration of others.

- Expressive people can sometimes go from highs to lows very quickly. Guard against gaining a reputation for being subject to mood swings. If others are unsure of your mood, it can build an unnecessary barrier.

- The ability to amuse or entertain others can make being with you fun and entertaining. While there is nothing wrong with having a sense of humor or being clever, make sure that other people can see that you're capable of serious, reflective communication. Being serious when it's appropriate will help build an image of reliability and competence.

- If you're overly exuberant, you're a roller coaster without brakes. Take some time to make sure your intensity level matches the occasion before you derail in manic excess.

- *Managers:* A person who is very high on the two E's may find difficulty in reaching executive or middle manager positions. This is because the higher you climb in an organization, the more you will know but the less you are usually supposed to say. Remember that with increased responsibility comes the need for increased discretion.

- *Managers:* The employee with this personality profile may move to action without reflecting, so it is wise to help him or her think things through by discussing the alternatives. Talking is a way of thinking too.
- *Managers:* If you're *in charge* of a meeting and an exhibitionist monopolizes the discussion, as soon as he takes a breath, jump in and thank him or her for providing input, then turn away. Avoid further eye contact and ask the group, "Who else would like to comment?" If the person still refuses to butt out, say, "What I would like to do is get everyone else's response before we get back to you." In this way, you have not only told the person what you expect of him or her, but now there is reinforcement from the group.

Low Exhibitionism and Enthusiasm. Are you generally more quiet and serious? Is high visibility within social settings a bit uncomfortable? Do you tend to have a more cautious orientation toward life? If so, you're probably low on visibility and enthusiasm. At the office, for example, you're likely to be seen as serious and dependable because you check and recheck work for mistakes. Supervisors probably see you as being responsible. And in meetings, you feel more comfortable discussing things which you are knowledgeable about rather than expressing an opinion on everything.

Is this apparent social hesitation a sign of insecurity or depression? Not necessarily. It really depends on the extent of a person's social hesitation and whether or not he or she is able to connect with people in other ways. You may, for example, not have a lot to contribute in the area of *general* conversation. When you do talk, however, your thoughts may be very deep and helpful.

Claire was a Wheaton College graduate who eventually became a congressional aide on Capitol Hill. She was a bright, petite, and pretty woman who was conscientious, quiet, and thoughtful. Her job was to study important issues, and then make recommendations to her boss, a state senator. A deep and reflective thinker, you could count on Claire to examine all sides of an issue and come up with penetrating insights in reference to a given situation.

Claire's background was part Scandinavian. She was raised in a tradition that emphasized correctness, logic, politeness, and a touch of "children should be seen and not heard." When you talked with Claire, you could tell that she was discreet about what she divulged, making sure that her remarks were well chosen and appropriate. Her boss, the congressman, appreciated Claire because he knew she worked hard and took things very seriously. One of the most difficult aspects of her job, however, was that periodically she was called upon to make presentations to groups. But because of Claire's reserved, quiet personality, she came across to others as too subdued and emotionless. The net effect of her presentations was not at all impressive. But even though Claire was not expressive in a group situation, she thoroughly enjoyed quiet, serious conversations with her closest friends.

Tips for Low Exhibitionists and Enthusiasts

• Your quiet, serious, and careful style may cause your co-workers to view you as unfriendly, negative, or not interesting. Effective work relationships require communicating a measure of enthusiasm and showing some interest in other people. Do a reality check to make sure you show an interest in your co-workers and that you're not spreading doom and gloom. A little humor in the office can often be just the right medicine to help relieve the pressures of the job.

• It's possible that you are cautious because you don't want to say the wrong thing and embarrass yourself. Forcing yourself to be the life of the party would probably be too stressful. When the boss is around, however, you may need to speak or ask questions in order to be recognized or heard. Managers are busy and they may not be inclined to take the time and energy to draw you out.

• An important part of some people's work is making good first impressions. When meeting others for the first time, make an effort to shine and sparkle, not holding back. If you tend to be introverted, your idea of being "larger than life" will probably come through about average in comparison with everyone else.

• *Managers:* Don't be too hasty to overlook the contributions that a low-key worker can bring to work. What they don't have in flash or charisma is often made up for in substance and depth.

• *Managers:* Sometimes you have to draw out low-key employees. Seek their opinions and ask for their input. Once they express themselves, remember to compliment them for their contribution.

THREAT SENSITIVITY: CAUTION VERSUS RISK

At work, some people need adventure and risk, others prefer to play it safe. When faced with situations that are physically or socially threatening, what is your first reaction? Fight or flight? The degree to which you are sensitive to threatening situations creates what I like to call your "risk setpoint." Public speakers, salespersons, airline pilots, firefighters, entrepreneurs, and convicted criminals, for example, tend to be less afraid of threatening situations. Elementary school teachers, accountants, quality control engineers, and proofreaders, as a whole, have a more cautious orientation to life.

Donald Trump is a great example of an adventurous risk taker. So is hamburger tycoon, Carl Karcher. An Ohio farm boy, Karcher took a risk in 1941 by buying a hot dog cart for three hundred and twenty-six dollars. Of that investment, three hundred and eleven dollars came from a bank loan! Today Carl Karcher Enterprises (Carl Jr.'s) is an empire of over six hundred restaurants and 14,000 employees. For every risk-taker, however, there needs to be some risk-avoiders to balance things out.

Our personality orientation of either caution or risk is also expressed in our work lives. My friend, Bill Bennett, is an entrepreneur from New Jersey who started a small advertising firm a few years ago with only a few dollars in his pocket. Over the last six years Bill has taken some considerable risks and his company has doubled many times in size.

Away from the office, Bill's personality is no less adventurous. Whether it's white water rafting, sky diving, or bungee jumping, Bill is rarely held back by "what if" kind of worries. This is in contrast to those who seem highly adventurous but are much more cautious. Last year, for example, Bill and I went bungee jumping off New Zealand's 230-foot Skipper's Canyon. Before and during the jump Bill had very few reservations. He just did it! Before I made the decision to jump, however, I interviewed half a dozen or more jumpers and discussed the possible dangers with an orthopedic surgeon. Bill, the quintessential risk-taker, makes more money than I do.

HIGH RISK-TAKERS

If you're a high risk-taker, you enjoy taking chances. Some might even call you reckless or a daredevil. You are willing to face uncertain outcomes. Speaking in front of a group of strangers or starting a new business would be more natural for you than for a low risk-taker.

Typically high risk-takers are adventurous, bold, energetic people who can withstand pressures fairly well. Their "strong nerves" allow them to cope well. However, they can be careless of details, ignore danger signals, and expect others to be just as venturesome. A high risk-taker in a mundane job will often do lots of things that are adventurous *outside* of work.

Tips for High Risk-Takers
- If your boss is rather cautious, the old adage, "It's better to seek forgiveness than permission" does not apply. If your boss doesn't delegate well, you may need to keep him or her posted on developments. From your boss' point of view, your risky ideas could backfire and endanger his or her job security. You may need to keep explaining the details many times to reduce your boss' anxiety.
- Depending upon the culture of your organization, your "gung-ho" style could make you either a hero or a villain. If your business is very conservative, you can be seen as a dangerous gambler. If the atmosphere is enterprising, you may be on the cutting edge. Ask yourself whether your personality style fits the

organization's profile. As a rule, smaller organizations tend to promote more individual creativity and risk-taking.

- Planning and organization are not high on the priority list for some risk-takers. As a company makes the transition from an entrepreneurial beginning to the professional management stage, these skills become increasingly essential.

- *Managers:* Help risk-takers think through the consequences of their plans and actions. Set limits regarding what they can and cannot do. Being clear about your expectations and boundaries will protect you from a lot of unanticipated problems and will also keep the risk-takers out of a heap of trouble.

LOW RISK-TAKERS

Do you tend to have a rather cautious outlook on most matters—emphasizing all the things that *could* go wrong? Do you often feel like withdrawing from social situations? Do you make a point not to draw attention to yourself? Is job security a high priority to you? If so, you're a low risk-taker.

Low risk-takers are generally discreet, cautious people who dislike unpredictable circumstances. They avoid situations of personal risk, even those that promise great rewards.

As a whole, low risk-takers excel in the more conservative types of jobs, such as money management, bookkeeping, quality control, or detail work that others may consider tedious. In these roles low risk-takers are often seen by their supervisors as superstars. Low risk-takers can also make important contributions to group decision-making processes because they entertain a universe of "what ifs" that others often overlook. However, when low risk-takers are placed in assignments that require that they be bold and larger than life, rather than throwing caution to the wind, they usually end up with sand in their eyes.

Roger, for example, was a finance specialist who, until he was promoted to the position of finance manager, worked in an office by himself. It was a very low-key job. After his promotion, Roger started getting stressed. For the first time in his life, he had six employees to manage and presentations to make to senior management. Roger disliked speaking in public. He also discovered that it was necessary to bargain and "schmooze" with other managers in order to get the support that he needed to meet his departmental objectives. Each month, Roger discovered that he had to pull rabbits out of hats in order to find the resources he needed to do his job. As a risk-avoider, Roger found the demands of his job to be nerve-racking and it wasn't long before he was overwhelmed and wanted out.

The cautious boss who supervises a low risk-taker will often feel very secure. A cautious boss who supervises a high risk-taker is often very fearful that the bold subordinate is going to do something that will jeopardize his or her position in the company. This is particularly true in large conservative organizations where innovation and risk-taking are often discouraged. But when the best and most adventurous employees are not given the opportunity to try new things, they often leave as soon as an opportunity presents itself.

Tips for Low Risk-Takers

- Others may appreciate you for your thoroughness and attentiveness to detail. But high risk-takers often tend to see you as frozen with "analysis paralysis." If your job calls for you to exercise leadership or make some quick decisions, be ready to move forward without undue hesitation. Your ability may be under question if you don't.
- If you have a tendency to be reluctant to try new things, your concerns could actually be rationalizations based on the fear of failure. You can start to put those fears into perspective by realizing that the worst possible outcome is often not that bad. Once you've done this, practice taking some small, calculated risks in order to bolster your confidence. The process usually becomes easier as you go along.
- Don't misconstrue risk-taking for gambling. When a business decision is based on facts, the odds are stacked in your favor. Without good information and wise planning, your likelihood of success is much smaller.

- Your cautiousness may have its roots in a low self-image. Learn to trust your own ideas and feelings. By becoming preoccupied with your fears, you are much more likely to make a mistake.
- *Managers:* When implementing change, give low risk-takers plenty of advance warning so they can be mentally and emotionally prepared. Also be sure to listen carefully to their concerns *and* allow them to express their feelings. Then give them plenty of reassurance. In the case of a major change, it is often wise to demonstrate something first on a smaller scale to show that it works before proceeding the whole way.
- *Managers:* You will need to watch a low risk-taker's tendency to overplan and hold back from completing assignments. If your business involves a lot of competition and the necessity of frequent changes, you will need to set specific deadlines. Otherwise, a low-risk person will spend all his or her time preparing to do a job that fails to get done.

SOCIAL PARTICIPATION

At work, people seek the company of others for a variety of reasons. People persons, as we discussed in the previous chapter, enjoy building personal relationships which stress warmth, service, and relatedness. Along these lines, some extroverts are indeed people persons. Other extroverts, however, seek social experiences, not for the warm fuzzies, but rather for information, excitement, and opportunities to influence people or gain personally.

Bob, for example, is about the most charming extrovert that you would ever meet. Highly insightful, he knows just what to say to get you to let your guard down. With a contagious smile, sparkling eyes, and a well timed laugh, you get the feeling that Bob is going to be your close friend for life. After Bob gets what he needs from you, however, you may never see him again because he merely uses people as a means to an end.

Joni, on the other hand, is both a warm people person and an extroverted joiner. Whether at work, at the health club, or at church, Joni loves to connect with people. Her warm, engaging smile, along with a large dose of exuberance and enthusiasm, makes her presence immediately felt. As a clothing salesperson for a large department store, Joni has won top honors for several years. Even though she could make more money in another job, it would offer fewer social contacts so Joni doesn't give much thought about changing her employment. There is just the right amount of people action in her present job.

Do you prefer work that offers plenty of social interaction or do you prefer to be left alone?

I recently gave a lecture to a group of young singles in Colorado Springs on the topic of finding the right job-to-person match for your future. When I raised the point about how people often make career decisions based upon their skills rather than their motivations and personalities, a woman raised her hand. She told the group that although she can type sixty words per minute, she will never again take a typing job because it left her feeling too isolated from other people.

High Social Participation. Do you have lots of friends and social contacts, belong to several organizations, go out often, and enjoy the company of others? Do friends and strangers alike see your outgoing side? Do you keep an active schedule and value personal contact? If so, you're a social "animal"!

Tips for High Social Participators
- A good occupational fit for you is a job where you can have considerable people contact. Avoid jobs that have insufficient social opportunities. Generally, you should try to avoid jobs where you are isolated from others. Working alone as a data entry operator, for example, would be extremely unfulfilling.
- Although time spent talking with people may make you well-liked or meet your social needs, it can also cause a problem by interfering with production and causing your colleagues to lag behind in other areas of their work. Resist the temptation to avoid unpleasant or nonsocial duties such as paperwork or

reports. Make developing better work habits and time management skills a greater priority.

- *Managers:* If you are a people person and need a lot of social stimulation, guard against spending too much of your subordinates' time. Make sure that you are not keeping your office staff from doing their work.

Low Social Participation. Individuals who like to keep social participation to a minimum are often very independent and high self-starters. They don't need others around to motivate them into action. On the other hand, it may be that they have never learned the art of forming close human alliances. Some may avoid social situations because they feel troubled about their own inadequacies. Still others may avoid social contacts because they are unable to control or influence others. A sense of diminished power causes them to want to retreat. Introverts such as the ones just described tend to participate in a minimum of group activities and avoid activities that involve much relating.

Tips for Low Social Participators

- If large social groups intimidate you, learn to smile when you enter a room and find one or two friends with whom you feel comfortable enough to talk. Standing by yourself in a conspicuous fashion will only exacerbate your feelings of social ineptness and cause others to classify you as a loner.
- Learn to be more observant of social subtleties. Sometimes there are interpersonal issues or political dynamics that must be understood if you are to be successful. Make it a point to probe deeper into the motivations of others rather than merely accepting every behavior of every co-worker at face value.
- When you are too withdrawn or aloof, you give the impression that you are not very interested in the company of others or would rather not be involved in friendly social relations. However, since you are not in a vacuum, and good working relationships require you to be at least minimally sociable, you need to force yourself to verbally communicate with others. Unless you

learn to communicate effectively, it could rob you of the impact or influence you want, and your ideas might easily be ignored. Refrain from giving very short answers. Learn to ask questions that will draw the other person out and get him or her to talk. The person will like you for that.

- Perhaps your disinterest in social relationships is rooted in a some lack of social confidence. You may actually think of yourself as a bit dull and boring. But even if you're unsure of what to say, you can always smile at people. A smile indicates friendliness. Then, share more of yourself. Let your sense of humor show. Talk about those things that energize and excite you. All of us have at least a few interesting stories to share about ourselves.
- If you are too quiet, aloof, or appear unfriendly, it may keep you from making a good first impression. Work to be more expressive, enthusiastic, energetic, cheerful, and outgoing when you are in the presence of others. This is especially important in the early stages of getting acquainted.
- *Managers:* If you're a low social participator, make sure that you invest enough time and energy in building solid relationships with your subordinates. Lack of positive feedback can lead your employees to believe that you don't care for them personally and that you are not pleased with their work performance. It can also cause them to feel that they are being used. As a result, staff morale can suffer and employee turnover may be high.
- *Managers:* In relating to a subordinate who is unsocial, don't assume that he or she is unfriendly or strange. Although the person's demeanor may be cool, it may just mean that he or she is a private person.

SUMMARY

Are you primarily an introvert or an extrovert? Most people fall into one category or the other as the major source of their energy. Although, as we have seen, extroverts may or may not be people persons, one thing is certain—they become charged by the electricity that flows from being with others. Introverts, on the other hand, are more comfortable pondering their own thoughts and doing their own things without the interruption of others.

How your job fits with your personal introversion and extroversion pattern will have a lot to do with the quality of your work life.

3

Of Power Plays and Power Brokers

Subfactors for Personality Pattern:
Assertiveness, Trust, Orientation to Change,
Self-Concept.

*P*OWER TIES, POWER WALKING, POWER MEETINGS, *power* lunches, *power* writing—the "P" word is trendy. For the purpose of understanding personality, *power* refers to the human need to control or influence people or things, so we can feel competent to act in our own capacity. As you will see later on in this chapter, the intensity of this need varies from person to person.

This is a good time to think about your own power preferences and how they relate to (1) the people with whom you work, and (2) how much control your job requires you to exert.

"Are there any unwritten rules that everybody in this company knows but doesn't dare to talk about?" This is an interview question I sometimes ask employees privately before leading an off-site team building retreat.

"Sure," whispered the engineer as he glanced from side to side, "don't butt heads with Bob, or you're history!"

As president and founder of a fast-growing engineering firm, Bob has successfully harnessed his rapid decision-making abilities, direct style, and high control needs into building a multi-million dollar organization from a small consulting business. His employees would say that Bob is good at making deals, competing, and pushing people to perform. Unfortunately, when Bob has to delegate, show compassion, accommodate to the needs of others, or listen, he is often seriously lacking.

"I don't have time to waste with you," is Bob's typical response should he become angered. The more I learned about the company, the more I realized that fear was Bob's favorite motivational tool: *You'll do it my way or you'll find yourself on the highway.*

Is Bob successful? In the short term, yes. There's been impressive growth. His quasi-military management style, however, is starting to cause employee turnover because Bob intimidates and doesn't listen to employees. At present, profitability has not suffered because the company is in a growth mode and when decisions must be made, Bob knows most of the answers. When his company grows larger, however, Bob won't know all the answers. At that point, he is likely to encounter some turbulent times.

As you can see, how a leader or boss handles power-sharing within an organization will greatly influence both employee satisfaction and the organization's own productivity. In recent years management specialists have given considerable attention to the importance of involving and empowering employees to make more of their own work decisions. This is based on the realization that a well trained and mature employee is better able to decide how to accomplish tasks or goals for which he or she is responsible than others who are less directly involved in the job. The reason why power-sharing is important is because a basic need of every employee is to have some influence over what takes place in his or her work situation.

To really understand and apply the dynamics of power to your personal work situation requires an understanding of the specific personality factors that comprise the power pattern. These include such factors as assertiveness, trust, innovation, and self-image.

ASSERTIVENESS

Are you a commando or a coward? More likely, you're somewhere in between the two extremes. A person's level of assertiveness has to do with how much pressure one is willing to put on other people in order to get one's own way. It's about winning. Highly assertive people can be very competitive and demanding. Their focus is on what *they* want rather than what *you* want. Less assertive people are generally more patient and accommodating. They're naturally compliant, agreeable, and less assertive and they hate to look like the bad guy. Someone who is both highly assertive and a people person will want to get *his or her* way while at the same time making the other person feel comfortable. Often, leaders and top producing sales persons will fit with this combination. Obversely, a highly assertive and straightforward person who lacks interpersonal sensitivities will often be perceived as a "bull in the china shop."

High Assertiveness. The assertive person is of the opinion that life's consequences are controllable rather than inevitable. According to this action-oriented mindset, if something bad happens, someone must be at fault for not controlling the situation. "Make it happen," is their motto, and when a highly assertive person is unable to influence a situation, he or she feels helpless, out of control, or resentful.

People who are high on assertiveness hold strong opinions on a wide range of matters, and they aren't looking to be convinced about the validity of their point of view. When a problem arises or a decision needs to be made, they want to solve the problem, make the decision, and bring closure to a difficult situation: *right now!* A person who is both highly assertive and high on the two E's will be tempted to solve problems by jumping at the first solution that presents itself because he or she seeks closure and is impulsive.

Highly assertive persons often have less defined boundaries between their own individual thoughts and wishes and the sovereignty of others. Put simply, they don't always understand where their noses end and someone else's begins. Persons who are strongly assertive may also lack understanding for anyone who doesn't go along with their ideas.

Occupationally, they tend do well in jobs that are competitive and require the issuing of orders or challenging other people's points of view. Salespersons, for example, overcome resistance and close deals, athletes compete, judges give sentences, and power brokers make deals. When a highly assertive person lacks sensitivity and blurts out what he or she thinks too often, such a person is considered offensive. But when a highly assertive person is astute and knows how to use tact, he or she is seen as polished and smooth. Consider the example of a marketing liaison named Dale who used his assertiveness to arrange an important meeting.

Dale worked as a communications director for a charitable organization in southern California. His ministry needed the help of a leading advertising agency that specialized in promoting nonprofit organizations. "My next three months are completely booked," said Norm, the agency's president and creative director, "I don't have one moment to spare."

"I can appreciate your position," said Dale, "but we really need to get going on some marketing projects now, and we've heard that you're the best. Couldn't you at least visit us the next time you consult with another client in our area?"

"I'd like to," reflected Norm, "but every minute from the time I arrive to the time I leave for the airport is completely taken."

"Norm, when you leave your client's office, how do you get to the airport? Do you drive yourself in a rental car?"

"Yeah, but I have to return it to the airport. What do you have in mind?"

"Could we do this? From your client's door to the airport is a good hour-and-a-half drive through the city in rush hour. I think we would both agree that the drive to the airport is pretty much wasted time. If you're open to the idea, I'd like to arrange a mobile meeting between you and our executive committee in an R.V. on your way back to the airport."

"What about my rental car?" asked Norm.

"I'll have a staff member drive it back and return it for you. That way you won't have to drive through Los Angeles during rush hour. Seriously, Norm, I think you owe us the opportunity to at least have this one meeting with you. After all, you're a legend in the marketing field. To whom much is given, much is required, right? What do you say—will you give it a try?"

Norm agreed to go along with Dale's innovative idea. En route to the airport, they got their meeting. An assertive person himself, Norm responded well to Dale's challenge. In fact, several months later Norm asked Dale if he would be interested in possibly joining Norm's agency. "We need guys like you who can make things happen," said Norm.

In considering the similarity between Dale and Norm, it becomes obvious that people with similar assertiveness styles often have similar expectations of each other. When dealing with other people whose assertiveness level may be quite different from yours, you may need to modify your approach. Here are a few suggestions.

Tips for High Assertors

- If you are a person who is highly assertive, make sure you are aware of and respect other people's personal boundaries. Trying to take control of matters that are not clearly your responsibility may create unnecessary resentment.

- If you are highly assertive, you may find it easier to tell or persuade other people than to take direction or *listen* to their ideas. While there is a time and a place for providing control, guard against making a habit of forcing your own agenda on others without allowing them to express their own ideas and suggestions.

- Speaking too forcefully can also be intimidating. Try lessening the intensity of your voice. Speaking confidently, yet *thoughtfully*, will help assure that your constructive ideas are fully conveyed, welcomed, and acted upon.

- If your assertiveness is combined with a smooth and polished style, be careful to avoid a reputation for being too "slick" or manipulative. Once people feel they've been used, it's hard to regain their trust.

- If you are highly competitive but also have a low self-image, guard against being taken in by those who only tell you what you want to hear—regardless of the truth.

- If you are a highly assertive person, you may think that others should be direct and high powered too. But in all probability this expectation may be unrealistic for many of your employees.

So during discussions, for example, you may need to draw out the other person by asking questions or restating what you see as the other person's point of view. This helps to prevent misunderstandings.

- *Managers:* Highly assertive employees are often quite headstrong and may lack clear boundaries. Your employee may start doing things that have nothing to do with your expectations and objectives. Make sure he or she knows the importance of staying on track and keeping within the guidelines in the way you expect things to be done. Doing this makes it easier to give directions to an assertive employee because he or she will be more prone to recognize your authority as the legitimate manager.

- *Managers:* Those who must work as support persons to highly assertive employees are apt to become stressed. To avoid the undesirable outcome of a high turnover, alienation, or frequent conflict, make sure that you provide a satisfactory way for the harried support person to reduce, release, or manage that stress. You may need to be available to listen, and then "stick up for them."

CRUSADERS

Get ready to be misunderstood. The *crusader* is someone who likes to tell others what to do in the name of being "helpful." A motive of service in one who is assertive can often be frustrating for both the crusader and the one he or she is trying to help. If you are a crusader, realize that you are likely to be misunderstood by the very ones you are attempting to help. They may think of you as intrusive and critical. In fact, they may resent your suggestions.

Obversely, the crusader's typical gripe is, "Can't they see I'm doing this for their own good? How can they be so ungrateful?" As a crusader, you may be completely unaware that your agenda for them does not match the one they have for themselves.

Low Assertiveness. Gary has a tendency to smile and say "yes" even when he really means "no." He is very polite and is well liked around the office. He seldom makes waves. As a maintenance engineer, his job involves fixing equipment and other things that are giving the employees problems. Each day, Gary has a tendency to take on too many projects at once because he doesn't want to upset anyone by not being obliging. Because Gary cannot turn down anyone's request, it wasn't long before someone in the organization gave him a walkie-talkie radio so that he could be summoned more easily. At the end of the day, he was so tired from overwork and his feet hurt so much, he would have to soak them in hot water!

Gary was in a bind. He felt that people were taking him for granted, but he found it difficult to confront them. Then he hit on a clever solution! Gary started complaining that his walkie-talkie was so heavy that it hurt his back and he stopped carrying it around with him. At last, he had a few moments in the day where he could be truly incommunicado. This arrangement worked for a short time until people started leaving stacks of messages on his

---

Working with a crusader can be a mixed blessing. Assertive and independent persons rarely get along well with crusaders who are intent on telling them what to do and how to do it. If a person is not very assertive, feels insecure, or needs to learn the ropes, he or she may welcome a crusader's help—at first. In time, however, the "beneficiary" will want to spread his or her wings and fly away. Because the crusader makes so many suggestions about everything, the one being helped may reach the point where he or she no longer appreciates it. People may welcome help—but not too much of it.

How do you get a crusader to back off? First, acknowledge that his or her suggestions are probably good, but being so direct doesn't work with you. The next time the

continued on page 62

desk. Gary still needed to learn how to say "no."

If you tend to be accommodating like Gary, others probably think of you as a very nice person. You're also swayed more easily by peer pressure and by those who are more assertive than you. The exception, however, comes when the nonassertive person increases his level of dominance because his role makes that behavior less threatening. A technical or subject matter expert, for example, may readjust his normal assertiveness style in situations where others cannot compete with the power associated with his knowledge, skills, or abilities.

In comparing the difference between high and low assertive persons that I have known, I've noticed some interesting contrasts. Low assertive persons are indirect about expressing their needs and opinions. Highly assertive persons expect others to lay their issues on the table. Low assertive individuals come to fewer conclusions about how things should be done around the office. Highly assertive people wonder why others don't have as many opinions as they do. Persons low in assertiveness are less interested in bringing closure to issues, while the highly assertive want to get the job finished so it will be off their minds now. What low and high assertive persons both want, however, is an opportunity to be heard and for other people to take them seriously.

---

crusader becomes overbearing you might say, "You're probably right, but I'd feel much better about it if you'd allow me to figure it out for myself." At this point the crusader may back off, become hurt or resentful. He or she probably won't understand your "lack of appreciation."

Look at yourself carefully. Try to evaluate whether you have crusader tendencies. If you do, you should make a conscious effort to be sensitive to your own boundaries and the boundaries of others. People don't mind being led, but are apt to balk if they feel shoved. Furthermore, it's not good for your own health to become so deeply involved in everybody else's problems. Relax! The whole world isn't on your shoulders.

Tips for Low Assertive Persons

- As one who is low in assertiveness, you are happiest when working in friendly, harmonious situations. Your reticence to talk about your ideas may mean that you are better suited for a participative work setting rather than a managerial situation.

- Every job requires a certain amount of power negotiation. If you don't speak up and lobby for your position, your co-workers may view you as weak and either knowingly or unwittingly try to take advantage of you. When discussing matters, large or small, don't back down without first raising a few pertinent questions; then insist upon satisfactory answers.

- Because your highly assertive co-workers like competition and conflict, they are very comfortable in pressing what they consider to be a good point. In fact, they often enjoy a lively argument with a colleague they respect. Keep in mind that your lower tolerance for conflict may mean that your definition of an argument is what the assertive person considers a discussion.

- You may go along with some practices that are questionable because you feel it will make you more socially accepted. However, the wise person will not compromise his or her values in order to win the approval of others.

- It can be very difficult to win a point with someone who eclipses you by being more assertive. Avoid the tendency to go along with someone just to get the other person off your back. When you feel that you have been pushed into a corner, the tendency is to retaliate in other, more subtle ways. This type of "guerrilla warfare" is known as "passive aggressive" behavior and is not fair play.

- *Managers:* It's not easy for employees who are low in assertiveness to deal constructively with hidden feelings of anger. They often stuff their feelings inside until they build up and finally explode. Once these "meek, quiet" people have reached the boiling point, they may unload in anger all the things that have been building up over days, weeks, months, and even years. Therefore, encourage employees who are low in assertiveness to express how they really feel about their work situations. They may need assertiveness training, or in severe cases, therapy (see chapter on emotional adjustment).

Bridging the Gap. Distinct differences in assertiveness between two people can create a power imbalance that disrupts communication. The highly assertive person is often frustrated by the way information seems to be withheld by someone who is less assertive. Conversely, the less assertive person may feel threatened by the notion of saying what he or she really thinks or feels. When there is an assertiveness gap between two people, sometimes an awareness of the problem is enough for both parties to accommodate each other's needs. In this scenario, the assertive person listens more and the more passive person learns to be more open and direct. Because not everyone is able to sit down and discuss the accommodation process, it's sometimes possible to bridge the assertiveness gap by finding a *symbol* to express needs rather than saying the actual words themselves.

Brandon, the scheduling manager on a petrochemical project, noticed from time to time that Jill, a scheduling engineer, had difficulty getting her performance chart analyses finished on time. When she became bogged down, however, Jill rarely spoke about her frustrations; it just took her longer. This concerned Brandon.

"Jill," he said, "I've noticed that over these past couple of weeks you seem to have had some difficulty with the new performance chart system. We really do need to get those in on schedule. Are there some parts that you don't understand?"

"No," Jill answered. But the same slowdown occurred the following week. Again, she was reluctant to ask for help.

Then Brandon got an idea.

"Say, Jill, I know I've been a little uptight about the performance chart situation. I got to thinking about a possible solution. Perhaps, just between the two of us, if you should get in a jam, you could move your clock from the left where you usually have it over to the right side of your desk. I'll get the message and I'll come by and help you. Sound okay?"

"Yeah, that'll be fine. I like that idea. I could really use some help. Thanks, Brandon!"

HIGH TRUST VERSUS LOW TRUST

A few years ago I became involved with Harvest Time Ministries, a half-way house in my home town of Pasadena, California. They have several homes where paroled prison offenders can live while trying to rebuild their shattered lives. The program combines both supervision and structure in addition to Bible study, prayer, hard work, and lots of encouragement from Sister Jackson and her staff.

Upon a few occasions I have administered vocational and personality tests to some of the program residents in order to help them consider some of their vocational options. It was interesting to observe that most of these ex-cons scored extremely high on the "suspicious" factor. When I brought that to one man's attention, he politely mused, "Dr. Narramore, there's lots of games goin' on out there. If you don't watch it, you're gonna end up being a chump."

The personality factor of suspicion versus trust is related to the power pattern because the less we trust others, the more we want to control things ourselves.

Low Trust. Are you often wary of others' intentions? Do you feel that most people would try to take advantage of you if you let them? Are you skeptical of people's motives when they do something nice for you? If so, your low-trust style indicates that you are cynical and skeptical, assuming that the intentions of others are generally dishonest or self-serving. Low-trust persons often question what others say or do and want lots of information about what is happening.

Several years ago I was asked to conduct a research project on employee attitudes in a three-hundred-million-dollar resort. The results were to be shared with the general manager. The purpose was to help top management understand why in certain departments there was an annual employee turnover of up to 200 percent. Through the use of opinion surveys and employee interviews, I was able to gain clarity on a number of the root causes behind this problem. Midway through the project, I met with the general manager for a "five-minute" progress report on my research.

"What do you think of our hotel, Kevin?" asked the man who commanded over seventeen hundred employees. "Well, Jack, it's one of the most beautiful hotel resorts I've ever visited," I told him, "but with an organization the size of yours, there are areas that are going well and others that are not running so smoothly." I was a little ambiguous in my answer because I didn't want to give Jack too many specifics until the research had been completed. I preferred to wait until I could present my full findings and, at that time, make my recommendations to him and his executive committee jointly.

"I guess you don't know me very well, Kevin," said Jack. "When I ask a question, I want a straight answer."

Fortunately, my colleague, Bill, was in the meeting too and saved the day. "To answer your question, Jack," said Bill, "You've got some major problems in several departments such as housekeeping, grounds, guest services, and several of your restaurant outlets. These areas will all be covered in depth in our meeting with you and the executive committee next month. In the meantime, is there anything in particular that you would like to know?"

Jack was relieved to know that we were "on top" of the situation.

Executives like Jack tend to ask a lot of straightforward questions. If you don't answer to their satisfaction, they tend to be suspicious that either you are not aware of what is happening or, worse yet, that you are hiding something. Sometimes an executive who is a bit suspicious is well able to detect the presence of organizational politics. "Indeed, there are a lot of games going on!" would be the typical observation from a suspicious executive. The irony of this observation is that it may be true. A person who is low on trust is often more tuned in to organizational politics and has learned to recognize "games." In the extreme, however, low trust can limit a person's career development because he does not encourage his co-workers and is reluctant to delegate.

Once I conducted a study of ministers who had difficulty breaking the 100-person mark in attendance at their churches. Interestingly, I found that the common denominator shared by these pastors was their low score on being able to delegate. Similarly, I am reminded of a division manager at the assistant vice president level of a large corporation who absolutely could not let go of projects. Eventually, he became so burned out that he was demoted to a staff level position. At the root of his problem was the inability to trust other people to do things right!

Another characteristic of low trust persons is that they may have a less than altruistic view of serving and helping others. Those who have had their trust violated or who have grown up in a world in which they experienced unfortunate circumstances are often not inclined to extend good feelings toward other people. Consequently, a person who is less trusting in his or her attitude toward others will be better at analyzing and making a critical examination of a situation, but less inclined to give others the benefit of the doubt.

Tips for Low Trusters

- Some jobs are well suited to people who are low on trust: parole officers, prison officials, quality control inspectors, private investigators, and executives in extremely political organizations. They are more adept at being alert to irregularities and wrongdoing. If you have a job that brings out your suspicious side, guard against becoming cynical and completely disillusioned with life in general. Keep in mind that not everyone is out to get you. Your inclination will be either to turn sour on people or to isolate yourself so that people are either "insiders" or "outsiders."

- If you're a suspicious person, your co-workers may feel uncomfortable around you and resent your scrutiny. After all, not everyone is saying bad things behind your back. A critical or mistrusting attitude can ruin work relationships.

- Stress management can be extremely helpful. Several medical risk factors have been linked with high suspicion populations. These include higher incidence of coronary heart disease and low back pain. If it's hard for you to sustain friendships at work or maintain personal intimacy in your home, you probably could benefit from professional counseling.

- *Managers:* If it's difficult for you to delegate, remember that too much intervention on your part may make others overly dependent upon you. Rather than delegating tasks, you may tend to "micro-manage" both your employees and their work. This can block an organization's natural growth. *Sometimes the best way to manage is to simply let others do their job without a lot of interference.*

High Trust. Do you view your co-workers as basically honest and well-intentioned? Are you usually willing to believe what people tell you? Do you assume the best about others even though they may not always meet your expectations? If so, you are probably high on the trust factor. You are inclined to give others the benefit of the doubt. Imagine a world without trusting people. We need trusters. Without them, who would be positive, friendly, or open? High trust individuals do well in a variety of occupations whose common denominator is a basic belief in being receptive and helpful to others. Because they let their guard down, they tend to believe in the good intentions of other people, which results in being liked and appreciated by others, and usually generates better work because they are in an atmosphere of encouragement. High trust persons are inclined to be adaptable to various life situations and are concerned about the welfare of others. Sometimes, however, they can be thought of as naive or gullible.

To illustrate this point, one has only to watch the television program, "60 Minutes," to learn about poor, elderly shut-ins (from Iowa) who routinely sign their life savings over to fraudulent telemarketing scoundrels. Closer to home, modern organizations are filled with villains who are just as evil, victimizing others who are just as gullible.

I am reminded of a business owner I once knew who hired a junior consultant to help him with the work. The new employee was trained in all aspects of the business and after becoming privy to proprietary company information, left the firm taking with him its list of clients, then setting up shop across the street. I guess the moral of this story is that those who accept too many things without questioning will soon get a reputation among their low trust colleagues for being an easy mark. If you have an unsuspecting nature, consider the following tips.

Tips for High Trusters

- Although you like to give others the benefit of the doubt, sometimes a co-worker may have a hidden agenda. In fact, there are some people who are unscrupulous (see the section on the "antisocial personality" in chapter eight). So, rather than accepting everything at face value, remind yourself to give some consideration to possible ulterior motives behind people's actions. "I'll get that report to you first thing Monday morning!" may not really be true when the speaker is someone who is habitually late in turning in reports.
- Trusting too much can set you up for burnout. Some people go into certain types of jobs with unrealistic expectations, only to become frustrated because they are betrayed by the very ones they were hired to help. Urban police officers and social workers, for example, have a high incidence of burnout on their jobs.
- If you feel that organizational politics are affecting your job status, but you can't seem to recognize what's going on, seek out a low-trust co-worker who understands the political dynamics of your workplace. Ask him or her to cue you in on "how things really work around here."
- If you have a low-trust boss who asks for a status report, telling him bad news can actually be a plus as long as you're working to remedy the problem and keep him informed. However, a simple positive response such as "just fine" may cause him to wonder if you may be "covering up" some problem, or if you're just out of touch with your assignment.

ORIENTATION TO CHANGE: INNOVATION VERSUS TRADITION

This subfactor of the power pattern has to do with a person's receptiveness to change. Those who are dissatisfied with the status quo often feel a need to control because they want things to be done differently—their way. For innovative persons, changes of many different types are not only expected, but almost a religion. But for those who are traditionalists, the anticipation of change is intimidating and fills them with concern. The degree to which these people accept or reject conventional ideas also influences a variety of areas including creativity, need for independence, quality of work relationships, and how long they will stay in an unrewarding job.

As organizations grow and mature, for example, they create more and more structure and become increasingly tied to long-standing traditions. This creates an increasing demand for employees to follow established guidelines. Whether it's the federal government or a Detroit automobile manufacturer, the size of the company and its traditions often creates an environment where new ideas are blocked. Lee Iacocca, for example, exemplifies a change-oriented executive who, stifled by bureaucracy, left the establishment (Ford) to run his own enterprise by becoming president of Chrysler Motors! An innovator, then, is apt to question authority, generate new ideas, and insist that his or her recommendations be implemented.

Traditionalist. Tradition-oriented persons enjoy the familiar and are often reluctant to make changes. Conservative in the classical sense, they tend to reminisce about the past and hold fast to the values they were taught as children. To them, job security, stability, and consistency are important. However, while a preference for tradition usually reinforces stability and structure, it also has a potential for stagnation and, in this way, can retard progress.

I once conducted some market research for an organization that offered professional seminars for local business persons. The meetings were held on a certain day of each week at eight in the evening. While interviewing a randomly selected group of people who no longer attended the meetings, I learned, among other things, that eight was an inconvenient meeting time. The individuals in my focus group much preferred either seven or seven-thirty in the evening.

When I presented the results to the organization's director he was a bit agitated. "We've always met at eight and I don't know if people could adjust to the new time." Speaking philosophically, he went on to say that "when you've been doing something one way for a long time, it's not good to make changes." When asked *why*, he didn't know. It just seemed to him that staying with the status quo was being consistent. Therefore, it was the right thing to do. Yet, after reflecting on his tendency to prefer the status quo, the leader decided to change the meeting time and was pleased by the increased attendance.

For traditionalists, holding blindly to tradition can impede an individual's willingness to adapt to much-needed change. When an organization is overwhelmed with too many traditionalists, it prevents progress and causes it to lose it's competitive edge. So keep in mind that if you are traditionally oriented, it's essential to periodically reevaluate your procedures to be sure you are maximizing your company's efficiency.

A boss who is high on tradition will often view a co-worker who is low on tradition as a "radical" who must be monitored to keep his "crazy" ideas from damaging the company. If you tend to be more on the non-traditional side, but you work for a boss who is highly traditional, make an effort to understand his or her values and motives. Protect yourself by letting your boss know that you will do nothing to cause him or her embarrassment. Put your boss's mind at ease by assuring him or her that any changes you make will bring praise, not criticism, to the organization. If you're proposing to make some major changes, keep in mind that too big a step at one time can cause a highly traditional person to panic and shift into reverse. If you are patient and are willing to go slowly, you are apt to be more convincing and your superior will be much more likely to let you carry out your creative ideas. But if you move too rapidly without adequate explanation, you may find yourself without a job.

Tips for Traditionalists
- In many organizations, if you are an employee who follows the established ways of doing things, you are generally viewed as dependable and loyal. Banking or manufacturing, for example,

usually reward those who follow the prescribed methods of doing their job.

- As a traditionalist, you must guard against the tendency to limit the creativity of others. This is especially important if you are employed in an organization that calls for innovation, new ideas, or artistic expression. Try not to establish a reputation for saying, "No, that won't work; we've tried it before." Just because it didn't work before doesn't mean that someone hasn't designed "a better mousetrap."

- You may find adjusting to change or coping with unexpected demands to be stressful. If you're going through a major change at work or at home, be sure you have a support system to help you. This could be comprised of one or more close friends, your pastor, a mentor, a psychologist, or a counselor.

- *Managers:* If you are high on tradition, your views may be reassuring to others in your organization who share them. However, if you are wise, you will avoid insulating yourself with a core of employees who are not creative or too intimidated to think innovatively. A board of directors or a strategic planning unit can often benefit from a "pot stirrer" who infuses the process of decision-making with fresh thinking and new ideas.

- *Managers:* Because you appreciate conventional ways of thinking, you may feel very comfortable with long-standing procedures involving rules and restrictions. In most work settings, too many rules can stifle personal involvement and restrict personal responsibility. It is better to give people basic boundaries and expectations, then reward them for their superior performance.

Innovators. Do you often think of different ways of doing things? Do you get upset with others who are not open to new ideas? Are you particularly broad-minded and divergent in your thinking? If so, you're an innovator. Your strong preference for original ideas indicates that you take very little for granted. You tend to be analytical, critical of old and new ideas alike, and are not swayed in your thinking by how things have "always been done" in the past. Some may see you as forward-thinking and creative, but others may view you as unconventional and a maverick. They may even think of your suggestions as being "off the wall."

Mack was a highly successful salesperson in the field of financial planning. People who knew him marveled at his uncanny ability to find a financial vehicle that would bridge an individual's money needs with his organization's programs. Back at the home office, however, Mack was a "thorn in the flesh." Why? Because every few months Mack would come up with a new idea for some "wonderful, fool-proof" financial program, and would lay on the pressure for the head office to adopt his plan. Because Mack was so successful out in the field, the executives acceded to taking Mack's calls and listening to his sales pitch. Sometimes, though, it got tiresome and they wished he would leave them alone and stop coming up with so many ideas. Yet Mack's insistence that his innovations be implemented was the very thing that ensured his successes. Innovators without the power to implement their ideas are like architects who never see their designs executed.

Tips for Innovators
- Innovators are often intolerant of the "tried and true" and tend not to think of formal organizational procedures as "sacred" or "untouchable." If you are innovative and are frustrated by the bureaucracy and restrictions of a large established corporation, it might be more rewarding for you to accept employment in a smaller organization where you will have more freedom. Or you might consider the route of being self-employed. For job satisfaction, be sure to seek a role that allows you the greatest amount of autonomy and decision-making relative to your ability and field of expertise.
- Highly innovative persons often find it hard to stay within guidelines or to compromise their ideas. For this reason, they sometimes receive negative performance ratings from their supervisors. It is imperative that you establish an amicable working relationship with your boss. This could mean praying for patience and counting to ten before speaking your mind.
- *Managers:* As one who is high on innovation, diplomacy is

critical if you are attempting to convince higher management that innovative changes should be made. Keep in mind that change is a process, and as such, may require time. Try to think what your ideas represent from the perspective of the ones you are trying to persuade. In particular, pay close attention to customs and traditions in your organization before setting out to make many changes. What stands to be gained or lost by the changes you are proposing?

- *Managers:* Although change is usually linked with progress, change for its own sake can be counterproductive. Unwarranted change can even produce unintended, negative side effects. Be sure that the changes you desire will actually represent a net improvement.

A Note about Self-Concept. Although a person's view of his or her own adequacy is a personality factor relating to emotional adjustment, it also relates to the power pattern. In particular, the two extremes of self-concept often have a direct effect on a person's desire to either (1) influence others, or (2) receive direction.

Those who feel confident about themselves will readily trust their ideas and feelings and, therefore, have a more frequent desire to obtain influence over others. When this trait is extreme, the person may be so overly confident that he or she refuses to listen to others and can be very difficult to work with.

On the other hand, a person who is low in self confidence and highly self-conscious will feel inadequate and embarrassed at the very idea of expressing his or her own opinions, which the person feels certain must be no good. Thus, extreme sensitivity to embarrassment is likely to cause the person to withdraw and prevent him or her from leading others.

SUMMARY

To improve the quality of one's work life, each person must come to terms with his or her personal need to either give structure or to receive it from others. Usually, a pattern established in our early years does not vary appreciably over a period of time. Recognizing your own levels of assertiveness, trust, orientation to change, and the strength of your self-concept are foundational to finding a work setting that's right for you. An assertive innovator, for example, would feel stiffled in a large bureaucracy where his or her ideas meet the resistance of deaf ears. A traditionalist, on the other hand, may enjoy work that offers established ways of doing things. Within your job, knowing your power preferences can be the first step to compensating for the blind spots that may accompany your strengths.

4

Can We Depend on You?

*Subfactors for Personality Pattern:
Rule-Keeping versus Rule-Breaking,
Direct versus Indirect Focus,
Concern for Order versus Laxness,
Impulsiveness versus Deliberation.*

A faithful employee is as refreshing as a cool day in the hot summertime. **Proverbs 25:13,** *Living Bible*

CAN YOU PUT ASIDE your own private needs in order to meet the demands of your job? Your reputation on the job is greatly influenced by your pattern of dependability.

Raymond, for example, had a combination of personality factors which took its toll on his work habits. It was 8:41 in the morning and he was barreling down the freeway trying to make it to the office in time. He was weaving in and out of traffic in the fast lane, half wondering why the other cars didn't all move to the right and simply let him by.

"I should have left twenty-five minutes ago," Raymond admitted with chagrin.

"Maybe if I keep it at eighty miles an hour, I can still get to work on time. It's not right to lie, but I better have an excuse in case I'm late again. Medical appointments are pretty believable, so are sick children. No, I used that last time. They won't believe me if I keep telling the same story each time. Maybe if I say I got pulled over by a cop, it would work. One of these days I've got to get a radar detector.

"Oh, I'd better shave. Clever idea—shaving in the car. Gives me five more minutes to snooze. Shucks, I forgot to clean the shaver head. No problem, I'll roll the window down and let the wind blow it out.

"Now, let's see—what do I need to do to get ready for this morning's meeting? Did I remember to spell-check my report? Boy, Dan sure gets uptight if things aren't just perfect. Going to work every day is such a ball and chain.

"I wish I owned the company. Then I'd arrange to meet with the area reps in Hawaii twice a year. No, I'd move our headquarters there or maybe I'd semi-retire! I wonder how hard it would be to find a part-time job in Maui?

"Man, freeway traffic is getting slower! I'd better get off the next exit and find an open side street. That way I'll avoid all this mess. Mmmm, there's a Winchell's Donut shop along the way. If they're fast about it, I would only lose 90 seconds.

"Now let me think—I wonder what my excuse should be?"

Raymond, although a fictitious character, is a composite of several people with whom I have consulted or actually known. As a case study, Raymond embodies a blend of personality factors which, when taken together, create an employer's nightmare.

Of course, this was not Raymond's first time to be late. In fact, he's habitually tardy. Among all his other flaws, Raymond is Mr. Impulsive. He is full of last minute, impractical urges, such as turning off the freeway and stopping for donuts.

How about Raymond's absent-mindedness—leaving for the office without shaving? His thinking is creative, but he isn't very focused. Raymond's contemplations bounce from one idea to another residing most often among coconuts and palm trees.

What about Raymond's lack of commitment and irresponsibility? He thought nothing of being late, missing obligations, then lying to cover it up. He didn't mind cutting corners to meet his goals, even if that meant doing something he knew was unethical.

Neither did Raymond have any compunctions about doing shoddy work. He couldn't remember whether he had used the computer spell-check on his report, and he was annoyed because his superior insisted on a standard of excellence. How about his general disorganization? To put it plainly, Raymond's life is out of control.

Consider how impractical and unrealistic Raymond is in his thinking. Stopping for donuts takes more than ninety seconds! And most people can't support a family, or even themselves for a sustained period of time, on a part-time job (especially in Hawaii) without being subsidized by a trust fund or benevolent family members. And as far as owning a company is concerned, that doesn't usually happen without hard work.

How about Raymond's general lack of drive? He wanted another five minutes to snooze. Of course, part-time work was preferred. Hawaii would be a great place to lie around on the beach.

Although Raymond's story may be somewhat extreme, it illustrates several personality factors that produce unacceptable work habits. To name some: his scatterbrained approach to work, his disorganized and impulsive thought life, and, in a more general sense, his lack of drive. Unfortunately these weaknesses in Raymond's personality added up to create an employee with very little self-control which, of course, makes him undependable. Our pattern of dependability influences most every aspect of our day-to-day work lives and includes how well we plan, create, organize and carry out our responsibilities. These same characteristics in the opposite extreme tend to show up in personality traits of rigidness, inflexibility, and compulsiveness.

Consider the following example of Carl's self-talk.

"I think Room 26 would come closest to matching the room space specifications required for next month's meeting—it's the cleanest too. About the meeting participants: The first set of notices were sent through inter-office mail two weeks ago. Just to be sure, I better send a second set to everyone's home address. That should be ample notice since I've already sent reminder memos to each of their department heads.

"During lunch this afternoon I'll have half an hour to spare, so I can go over the meeting notes again. In fact, I should time my comments with a stopwatch just to make sure I've estimated the time correctly. It wouldn't be fair to the others to allow the meeting to run over. I like things to end promptly at the scheduled time. I've earned a reputation for promptness, and I intend to maintain it. For that matter, I should probably ask the other presenters to time their presentations too.

"Oh, and if they have graphics, I'd like to see them ahead of time to make sure they're all appropriate. Some of those junior execs don't take their job very seriously. Rather than run home at five on the dot, why don't they ever think of giving something back to society? They could organize a drive for United Way or at least volunteer to be a floor monitor.

"About tomorrow, I should start packing for next week's trip. It's just an overnighter, so one bag should suffice. I wish those shuttle vans were more on time like they promise. It's not right to make people wait. I guess I should plan on arriving at the airport two hours before departure; you never know about traffic or other situations that might arise these days. What can I do to use that time well? Am I wasting time now?"

Carl, like Raymond, is an extremist. Carl's excessive control of his own behavior makes him a rigid, although dependable employee. His boss could conceivably try to harness Carl's rigidity in order to produce the work of three men. This is the "take them for all they've got" school of exploitative management. On the other hand, can you imagine the prospect of working next to Carl as a co-worker for an extended period of time? For some, Chinese water torture would be a preferred alternative to working with Carl.

These two examples are studies of opposing personality types. Carl is as committed to keeping every jot and tittle of every rule as Raymond is lax about rule-keeping. Carl's thinking style is aware and down-to-earth, Raymond's is creative and absent-minded. Carl is fastidiously concerned about correctness, Raymond could scarcely care less. Carl is intensely pragmatic, while Raymond is downright unrealistic. Carl restrained; Raymond, impulsive. Let's look at each of these qualities separately.

MORAL CONFORMITY: RULE-KEEPING VERSUS RULE-BREAKING

In the previous example, Raymond couldn't care less about following society's rules such as being truthful and punctual. As you might guess, he would rate low on a dependability scale. Carl, on the other extreme, finds tremendous satisfaction in being responsible to the "nth" degree. In fact, he is so conscientious that he doesn't just go the second mile in carrying out an assignment—he goes the third and fourth as well. And he is meticulous about every detail. "Fussy, Fussy," his colleagues call him. Needless to say, Carl and Raymond wouldn't view each other with much warmth or empathy. Individuals who differ widely on the rule-keeping continuum often judge their opposites very harshly. Police officers, for example, sometimes refer to criminals as "scum-bags." Speeders, on the other hand, resent the "cold hearted" cop who writes a citation, reasoning that he must be on a "macho ego trip."

Businesses differ in their rule-keeping styles too. Large, bureaucratic organizations, for example, have lots of regulations and standard procedures. They have rules for everything and impose massive structure, rewarding those who follow them to the letter. A person close to the Carl end of the spectrum would feel very comfortable in this type of organization. Raymond, on the other hand, wouldn't last a week. However, smaller or more entrepreneurial firms often break with convention and enjoy the maneuverability that their more manageable size allows.

Rule-Keepers. Do you pay your bills on time and make a point never to exceed the posted speed limit? Do you return phone calls promptly and follow through on things to which you're committed? Do you find the prospect of going through *unofficial* channels to make arrangements repugnant? If so, you're a rule-keeper—someone who places a high value on doing the right thing and going by the book. Rule-keepers often do well in jobs that require great responsibility combined with the need for order. Airline pilots, accountants, certain types of religious workers, military cadets, judges, and police officers tend to be good examples. In these jobs, individuals have a great respect for following the letter of the law.

How well a person keeps the rules relates directly to his or her moral and ethical sensitivities. A person who lives by a Judeo-Christian belief system, for example, may be more inclined to follow moral imperatives than someone who has not been socialized by those values. This type of moral sensitivity becomes apparent when I speak to church groups about career-related issues. Often I hear laments from the audience about the difficulties of working with unethical, dishonest co-workers. I remember a specific complaint from a woman whose office manager would routinely clock-in absent employees who were the office manager's relatives. The nonfamily members at that office had a difficult time staying positive in the face of such flagrant rule-breaking.

Extremes in rule-keeping, however, can cut both ways. As Raymond and Carl illustrated, not only can people be irresponsible in their attitudes toward standards, but in some cases, they can be so extreme that they not only expect too much of themselves, but they are overly strict and judgmental of others. High rule-keepers follow the letter of the law and see most things as either black or white, and they miss all the color. They're the ones who get upset should you even consider taking the tag off your mattress!

Although their sensitivity to doing "the right thing" is usually positive, in some circumstances, rule-following can actually lead to an avoidance of responsibility. Carl, for example, was probably more concerned with following the time limit of the meeting than he was with the content of their discussions. The quality of the meeting wasn't his responsibility or concern. Legalism can sometimes create blind spots.

Although people differ in their backgrounds and mores, any thinking person will have to agree that moral laxness has completely permeated the latter part of the 20th century—including the work place. Employee theft in America, for example, has reached epidemic proportions. Corporate security experts report that employee theft is much worse than customer theft.[1] A manager I knew used to jokingly say that his department paid "five twenty-five an hour, plus all you can steal." He was only half joking. In our anything-goes society, which vehemently resists following any absolute moral code, rule-keepers are too often viewed as old fashioned prudes and sadly, are no longer respected as loyal and trusted employees.

Tips for Rule-Keepers

- While it's good to have high standards, resist the pitfall of being overly critical of your co-workers when it's not your job to straighten them out. The way to win the respect of co-workers is to "walk the talk" by being an example of your closely held values. This does not mean that you shouldn't speak your mind, but do it with discretion and tact. Wisdom from the Bible puts it this way: "Let your conversation be gracious as well as sensible, for then you will have the right answer for everyone" (Col 4:6).

- A good job fit for you may be an organization that is duty or cause-driven where high ideals are part of its ideology. Conversely, a company where ethics and values are often ignored will be a continual point of stress for you. When considering a new job, meet with a couple of employees informally and ask questions such as: "How do things *really* work around here?"

- Don't follow rules blindly. Ask yourself whether regulations and procedures are still accomplishing their intended purpose. Be aware that some organizational policies may have outlived their intended purpose and are actually counterproductive and need to be changed.

- When making decisions, rule-keepers sometimes get into the rut of oversimplifying things into black or white, either/or categories. You may be missing subtle nuances that others see. On important matters, discuss your perspective with a friend in order to get a "reality check."

- If your performance evaluation is tied to a co-worker who is a rule-breaker, make sure to distance yourself from that person. Otherwise, your reputation will be on the line, too.

- *Managers:* Just because you play by the rules, don't expect everyone else to be so conscientious. Remember that there are always some unscrupulous people who will do what you consider to be unthinkable—so be ready to deal with or replace employees who are not trustworthy or honest.
- *Managers:* If you're a strict rule-keeper, keep in mind that sometimes a "free thinker" can actually benefit an organization by helping it to break free of myopic, noncreative ruts. While unethical behavior should not be condoned, don't underestimate the value of a person who enjoys trying his wings by venturing outside the established order.

Rule-Breakers. Do you like doing things that other people say can't be done? Did you underreport your income tax on last year's 1040? If it meant not being late for an extremely important meeting, would you drive through a red light? Is "making it happen" more important to you than going "by the book"? Do you tell people what they want to hear in order to get what you want? If so, you're a bonafide rule-breaker.

To the rule-breaker, other people's expectations don't matter. In fact, beating the system is like a game. Along with beating the system comes a tendency to circumvent convention, to think innovatively to see how much you can get away with and to devise solutions to problems that others would never entertain. Extreme rule-breakers are often expedient, self-centered, and may even be psychopathic.

At the workplace, rule-breakers face an ongoing challenge of valuing expediency over honesty and integrity. To extreme rule-breakers, the idea of personal integrity is a foreign concept. So is being honest in all matters and putting in a "fair day's work for a fair day's pay." Why do rule-breakers buck convention and throw social mores to the wind? Sometimes they are expressing deep unresolved feelings of anger. Or they may break rules because they have a poor sense of personal boundaries or an overinflated sense of self. Still others may have a callous disregard for the rights and feelings of the other person. Rule-breakers feel that it's *their* life, so they're going to make their own choices. To them, your advice seems naive, puritanical, or out of touch with the way he or she sees the world turning today.

Although organizations tout their high ethical ideals, many businesses actually reward rule-breaking behavior because they see it as the only way to stave off the competition. Mixing a little bit of "we care" along with "nice guys finish last" is a double message that can be extremely confusing and even alienating to some employees. If you are the leader of an organization and you want the public to assess your business as one who lives up to it's commitment to integrity, consider whether you are really "walking your talk." That is, consider your own example of honesty, ethics, impartiality, and fairness. Second, make sure that you have a consistent procedure for rewarding ethical behavior and punishing unethical behavior.

Tom Dorstch of Compass Learning Systems Inc. says this about making values stick:

> Organizations are run more on symbols and what happens in crisis situations than anything else. My advice to a boss or head of an organization with unethical employees who are creating problems would be to say, "We're not doing this any more," and get rid of the first guy who crosses the line. The best thing you can do is make a very symbolic move right away and stick with it. Hopefully the message will get out about "what counts around here." Until you state what your values are and really live up to them—not just state them—but have real rewards and consequences, I don't think that you can control the person who is low on rule-keeping. He'll keep working the system.

Tips for Rule-Breakers
• If you tend to ignore the rules, realize that in rule-bound organizations you may be walking on thin ice. Make sure that you don't become calloused to the values and expectations of your organization. Are you on time for meetings? Do you follow through on promises? Be careful about your reputation. What

appears to be right to you may be unacceptable in your organization.

- If your boss is a rule-keeper, guard his or her reputation at the office by learning what his or her expectations are. What seems fine for you may be a cause of great concern for your boss. The phrase "It's better to seek forgiveness than permission" does not apply when your boss is your rule-keeping opposite.

- If you have an expedient side and are fortunate enough to recognize it, spend some time thinking about the experience in your life that caused you to become that way. You may need to build a new reputation. If you've mistreated or offended a co-worker, seek forgiveness and restitution. Similar to the approach of Alcoholics Anonymous, find a support system to help you and hold you accountable. Many organizations, especially churches, have support groups for business persons.

- *Managers:* Being on time to appointments and meeting your obligations becomes more and more important as your career progresses. If you fail to keep your word or break promises, your co-workers will lose faith in your ability to be trusted with important jobs.

- *Managers:* If you're a rule-breaker, be careful not to ask rule-keepers to accomplish the impossible. Your view of "anything's possible" may be very different to the steady worker who wants to plod along using "the same old standard way."

FOCUS: DIRECT OR INDIRECT

I've always been amazed at the way two people can look at the same object and see it altogether differently. One person's napkin is another person's notepad. One person's uncertainties are another person's playground of possibilities. The focus factor has to do with which mode of perception a person tends to favor while doing his work. A person with an immediate focus pays attention to the practical, "down to earth" matters of the moment and usually avoids anything "far-fetched" or unconventional. The other mode relies more on inner ideas and creativity that is often unrelated by association—even if on a subliminal level. As a continuum, the two opposite styles have to do with the immediate and practical versus the imaginative and absent-minded trend of thinking. Someone with the latter style will often be lower on the dependability pattern because the person is drawn away from work by so many distracting thoughts and ideas.

Indirect or "Unfocused" Thinking. Do you forget appointments or misplace important papers? How long does it take you to find your car in a shopping mall parking lot? Has the auto club canceled your subscription because you've called their locksmith too many times? Perhaps you're presenting a report and you've forgotten to include a crucial point—and you've already proofread the report twice today! Do you forget to bring materials to meetings or to finish work that you've been assigned until your boss or co-workers get angry? If you can answer yes to some of these questions, you are probably an indirect or "unfocused" thinker. (People who are not as kind or understanding may call you "scatterbrained.")

Unfocused people report that they are forgetful, misplace things, lose track of time, and do not notice what is obvious to others. Is there a link between such absentmindedness and lower intelligence? Or is it an indicator of genius? The answer to both is no, but if your focus is highly associative, you may be labeled unfairly. (People who are kinder and more generous in their analysis may think of unfocused thinkers as "dreamers.")

Being unfocused makes you neither a "good" or "bad" person, so don't feel guilty if you fit that category. You just process things in a different way. The truth is that associative thinkers are often highly creative and imaginative because their contemplative and dreamy style is what enables them to link together ideas that others would never have connected. Inventors are often associative in their patterns of thinking.

Occupationally, highly indirect or associative individuals may do well in academic, artistic, and many scientific endeavors. These include jobs such as artists, teachers, school counselors, university administrators, and writers—just to name a few. Routine jobs such as manufacturing, nursing, clerical work, law enforcement, and sales—which often call for attention to detail, alertness, and good memory—are often less successful fits. If you're unfocused and you're in one of these professions, you may do fine—as long as you have someone else to help you stay on track.

Consider the confessions of an absentminded executive named Paul: "I can hit one thought and then I can run off in any of ten different directions. All of them are great ideas to me at the time. I had a guy working for me, David, who was *not* absentminded. He was very focused! What I would do is give him assignments, or make suggestions, or ask him to do things. And every one of them was serious to him.

"About every three or four weeks David would come to my door and say, 'I can't take any more, I'm overloaded!' I'd say, 'David, bring your stuff in.'

"David would bring in a stack of work that I had given him and I'd start going through the stack and I'd say, 'David, this is very important and I want you to do this, but this other thing can wait for a couple of weeks.... Oh, I'm sorry.... Did I forget to tell you I don't want this one any more?'"

At work, however, indirect or associative thinkers are often unappreciated. Their lack of attentiveness to their surroundings caused by their inner preoccupation is often misunderstood as a lack of intelligence, unreliability, unfriendliness, and aloofness—or just plain laziness. It is not uncommon, for example, for an associative thinker to forget the day or time of day—let alone an important business meeting or deadline. If the indirect thinker has a track record of hitting home runs, all is forgiven. On the other hand, the scattered person who doesn't deliver rarely gets forgiven for his "eccentricity." Successful businesses are designed to meet goals.

Tips for Indirect or "Unfocused" Thinkers
- You need the type of employment that will pay you to think creatively. Too much structure or regimentation will force you to seek satisfaction outside of work.
- Associative thinkers often start their day with good intentions, but are easily sidetracked by a steady flow of new ideas. If your thoughts and energies tend to take on too many directions, dis-

cipline yourself so that you stay on target with your deadlines. In business, it's essential that you meet time demands and keep commitments since others are depending on you in order for them to do their jobs. One falling domino causes many others to tumble. Know the time limits so you don't stray too far from an assignment.

- If your boss wants something specific, be careful not to "change the order" unless you have his or her approval. In all but the most flexible organizations, if you deliver something other than what is expected, you're in trouble.

- Before you actually start work on a project, spend some time planning and attending to necessary details. It will save you time in the long run. Guard against momentary distractions. If this is difficult for you, consider taking a course in time management. It could help you both personally and professionally.

- Consider asking someone to help you get organized. Find some- one who will work with you in establishing a filing system, then reserve a certain time each day to file your paperwork, mail, and correspondence. You'll be able to find things when you want them. A good "daytimer" can help, too. Keep lists and check off items when you complete them. You'll feel great afterward!

- *Managers:* An unfocused employee needs a sense of structure and boundaries. Be careful not to overload a subordinate with too many work assignments without prioritizing them first. Also, ask a more focused employee to take care of details which you yourself might forget.

- *Managers:* If you are the creative type who tends to be unfo- cused about many details, a highly organized assistant can be a tremendous asset. Also pay attention to the needs and work progress of your subordinates. Set goals with them and schedule regular meeting times to check on their progress and to see what resources they might need from you. Write things down, but be sure to keep what you have written in a place where you can find it.

Direct Focus. Do you have a great memory for facts? Do you remember all kinds of details? Are your thoughts directed along realistic lines? Perhaps you are good at working with machinery. Are you diligent about watching every move and avoiding a possible accident? Persons who have immediate focus are often intensely practical and alert to their immediate surroundings. They're good at figuring out how things work and can usually operate machinery with ease. Their undivided focus is on the external world of the senses. What they may lack in inner imagination, they make up for in practicality, awareness, and common sense.

Occupationally, they are often found among the ranks of mechanical or procedural jobs such as bank managers, plant supervisors, engineers, mechanics, fire fighters, flight attendants, geologists, electricians, and police officers.

They also tend to have a fantastic memory for facts and details. Consider my friend, Randy, who operates heavy equipment for Cal-Trans. Randy was a group member of a recent adventure tour that I led to New Zealand. We both took a ride in a vintage biplane that featured a lot of aerial acrobatics. The maneuvers were thrilling, but the weather was choppy, and we both "lost our lunch." After the ride was over, however, Randy could remember every single one of the pilot's maneuvers from inverted 8's to 360's to barrel rolls and reverse stalls. All I could remember about the ride was moaning, "Oh boy, oh boy..." and then somehow making it back safely to the tarmac. A month later, however, Randy could remember every single maneuver like it had just happened.

At work, Randy is the same way. He remembers every single chunk of asphalt on the highway and is so mechanically gifted that he can drive almost any piece of heavy equipment that moves. Fortunately for the many motorists in southern California who drive on the 210 freeway, Randy perceives reality in a direct and immediate way—he pays attention to the road.

Tips for Those with Direct Focus
• Because you have a good memory and are alert to what needs to be done, your supervisors and co-workers will probably appreciate your dependability. A job that calls for maintaining and running an existing operation where procedures and policies are clearly defined is probably a good job fit for you. You may also

do well in detail-oriented jobs such as proofreading. Jobs requiring innovation and creative thinking like advertising, writing, or academics, for example, may be more of a stretch.

- The business world is concerned with total quality. If your boss is not exactly a detail person, you may be a tremendous resource both to him or her and the organization. Since you're good at details, you may want to find an influential person and exercise your skill by helping him or her become even more successful. This won't do *you* any harm either.

- As a detailist, learn to think beyond the obvious facts that you observe. Seeing the big picture means going beyond the "how" questions to thinking theoretically about the "why."

- In job interviews and in situations where you need to make good first impressions, guard against coming across as a flat or nonexpressive nit-picker. In these situations, force yourself to be "larger than life."

- *Managers:* If you are detail oriented, be careful not to stifle the imagination of others who must do the creative work. Give creative employees clear expectations and limits, then give them a certain amount of leeway to perform.

- *Managers:* If an employee is detail oriented, make sure you show appreciation for the way he or she catches the little errors that might otherwise slip through. Be sure, however, that the employee knows which assignments are of major importance to you and which are minor. That will help him or her allot work time accordingly.

CONCERN FOR ORDER VERSUS LAXNESS

One has only to think of Felix and Oscar of the "Odd Couple" television program to gain an immediate sense of the contrasting dimensions of concern for order versus laxness. At work, Oscar's desk was littered with papers, magazines, newspapers, receipts, lost tickets, and bits of old food. Felix's desk, on the other hand, might be found with one thing on it—a pen, positioned with perfect symmetry.

Those who seek precision and order are frequently concerned with living up to some very high personal standards. Punctual, reliable, and responsible, they often rate very high on dependability. Those less concerned with order are more casual, lax, and are less inclined to push themselves in order to obtain a self-imposed ideal.

Concern for Order. Is your office neat, tidy, and well organized? Is presenting a socially correct public image important to you? Are your emotions well under control? Are you quite methodical? Do you always try to produce work that you can be proud of? If so, you would probably score high on any psychological scale measuring a preference for order and correctness.

Your preference for order indicates that you are a disciplined person who likes to plan and use time effectively. You're proud of finishing your work on schedule without giving in to distractions. You're orderly and methodical. When you have a problem, you approach it systematically.

Those with a compulsion for order often focus on maintaining a socially approved self-image. The character sketch of Carl, for example, illustrates a person who spends an excessive amount of energy planning a meeting well in advance in order to avoid the embarrassment of being unprepared. If you have a moderately strong need for order, you're probably quite popular with your boss and your co-workers. After all, others don't have to push you to do your work because you are a self-motivator.

Tips for Those with a Concern for Order

- Your preference for orderliness and correctness means that you will naturally plan ahead on your projects. In moderation, this is as an excellent leadership trait; in the extreme, it can produce obsessive thoughts and actions such as compulsive neatness or workaholic behavior that might actually interfere with your success. Seek balance and perspective. Learn when it's time to end one project and begin another.

- Given your strengths, one road to success is to find a rising star in your company who needs help in being organized and staying that way. Your assistance may be rewarded as this person moves up the company ladder and sees you as part of his or her success.

- Your interest in always striving to do and say the correct thing may make it difficult for you to relate to others on a more friendly basis. Although businesses are task oriented, some work settings call for casual and informal communication. Decide to worry less about saying the appropriate thing. Be yourself and don't be afraid to relax a little.

- A popular scorecard for achievement is prestige. If you over-emphasize your good works, your co-workers may view you as smug, self-centered, or even arrogant. Try not to flaunt your achievements or status any more than is necessary. Let them find out about them on their own.

- If a co-worker does not share your same high standards and work expectations, it may cause some disagreement over what is acceptable in the quality of your work. Front-end communication in this area is important especially if the two of you are being jointly evaluated.

- *Managers:* If you are orderly and precise, watch that your perfectionism does not become a negative. Often it's helpful, but it can also become a compulsion that can turn people off and waste valuable time. Some tasks are more important than others. Guard against giving 100 percent to a project that should only require 20 percent of your time and energy.

- *Managers:* In supervising orderly employees, praise them for the excellent quality of their work but also encourage them to enjoy their work. Cultivate a sense of humor, and even playfulness, among your staff from time to time.

Laxness. Do you feel relaxed and self-satisfied most of the time? Do you often give in to urges of what you *feel* like doing as opposed to what *needs* to be done? Is maintaining a correct public image *not* very important to you? At work, do you sometimes dress a bit carelessly or express yourself in a vague manner? Is your career progression a bit haphazard? If so, you tend toward laxity rather than order—but you probably already knew that. To everyone else your office may look like a total disarray, but you're not bothered because you're comfortable with ambiguity and you can usually find things when you need to. As a disorganized friend of mine said, "I know where everything is. It's somewhere in my office!"

To the extreme, the lax person may be an undisciplined, unmotivated underachiever. On the other hand, some lax persons are very successful in certain artistic professions where it is advantageous to let things "hang loose." More frequently, however, the lax person just doesn't push himself or herself enough to achieve goals. Consider Jon who came to my office for vocational counseling.

After trying six jobs in the last eight years, Jon was not sure what he should try next. A middle-aged man who was balding, overweight, and a so-so dresser, Jon did not make the best first impression during an interview. When asked what job-leads he might have, Jon remembered that his brother-in-law had made a contact with an accounting firm that he could call. Upon this recollection, however, Jon's face turned sad as he remembered that he never showed up for the appointment that his brother-in-law had arranged. Jon's personality was so extremely undisciplined that he reminded me of a house on fire—without a smoke alarm to warn of impending doom.

Tips for the Lax

- People who are not constrained by the need for social appropriateness often have lower personal standards. If you want to make a good impression, make it a point to come to work appropriately dressed and groomed. How you present yourself sends a strong message to others about your reliability, consistency, and respect for others.

- Your more relaxed view of yourself may cause you to be ambivalent about who you are and what you want to do as your life's work. Avoid putting off important career choices. The more you postpone making choices, the more limited your options will become. Why, for example, should a company hire you when another applicant is ten years younger, just as smart, has gone ahead and gotten an education, and has more drive?

- You may have a tendency to procrastinate and produce careless work. Guard against gaining a reputation for having a lack of ambition; otherwise, you may be passed up for a promotion—or even the first on the list to go if the company has a need downsize. (And don't expect a glowing recommendation when you're looking for another job.)

- Your lackadaisical attitude of "anything goes" and "I'm not goin' to push myself" may have been learned from your home environment. However, a medical doctor can give you some tests to see if your problem might be a physical difficulty. For example, if you are struggling with a chemical imbalance or a thyroid deficiency, the right medication could make you feel "rarin' to go."

- *Managers:* your subordinates will interpret your lax attitude as permission to let their commitments slip. Why should they toe the mark, if you don't?

- *Managers:* If you have employees who tend to be lax, it's up to you to hold them accountable for their actions. You'll do them no favor by covering for them. It's also important that you encourage such employees by helping them set goals and follow through with their work assignments. By being definite about your expectations, you can help them learn to keep to a schedule.

IMPULSIVENESS VERSUS DELIBERATION

Another important factor that relates to dependability has to do with how well a person can control his or her impulses. On the job, this refers to a person's ability to carry out assigned tasks without giving in to distractions and disruptions in thought. Highly deliberate people are the ones who write the computer manuals; highly impulsive people are the ones who buy the computer, plug it in, start using it, and hope that somehow everything will work. The impulsivity factor is very similar to the two E's in that those who are the more exuberant and enthusiastic are often also the ones who tend to bore easily and therefore seek excitement and change. They also tend to be impulsive.

The impulsive person may not necessarily be enthusiastic and expressive. He or she will, however, tend to jump in with a minimal amount of information rather than weighing the pros and cons before taking action. The deliberate person, on the other hand, will collect substantial information and take plenty of time to process the data before making most decisions.

Impulsive. Do you make a lot of spur-of-the-moment decisions? Do you get easily sidetracked? Do people describe you as excitable, even rash? In most things, do you prefer to be more of a generalist than a specialist? Do you go on whims? If so, you're probably quite impulsive. Impulsive persons tend to act on their thoughts and feelings immediately, make decisions rapidly, and then change their minds or their moods just as quickly.

Impulsive persons tend to "binge-purge" when they are assigned a job. They'll start on the project until they feel antsy, rationalize that they have at least made a stab at it and now feel that they have earned a break. They'll relax and even do other things until they feel guilty about not working on the project. Then they'll come back and labor on the job until they again feel bored. Before you know it, they're caught in the "binge-purge" guilt cycle.

"I'm calling from a small country in Africa," whispered Kent, who was supposed to be in the United States writing research papers and attending classes at a prestigious Ivy League school. "You're not going to believe this, but I've been staying with the people at the American Embassy here. I'm using their phone line free of charge—can you believe it? Hey, would you mind calling the registrar's office for me and finding out what I need to do in order to apply for an incomplete? I've decided to spend a couple of days in Spain, too."

Although Kent was bright, charming, and very talented, he just couldn't overlook an "opportunity." The problem was, Kent saw everything as an "opportunity" that couldn't be missed. The hardest thing in the world for him was to stay on track. Every month or two, Kent would suddenly disappear for a few weeks, and his professors were starting to resent his excuses. It wasn't long before Kent was kicked out of graduate school. His employment history was not much different. If Kent could have stayed on course, he could have gone far and done well.

The positive side of being impulsive is that you don't mind being fluid and can change direction with ease. But if you are employed in a business that requires constant action, you must stay with the flow. If you don't, you'll find that there are consequences. Many successful entrepreneurs, for example, have a style of "shooting from the hip." I've met several business owners, for example, who have reflected "If I had thought about it twice, I would have done things differently."

Tips for the Impulsive

- Try to avoid tasks that require you to analyze too much detailed information. Your strength lies in seeing the big picture rather than focusing on individual details.

- You may not feel the need to plan. Guard against leaping into a task or a business enterprise with only a gut instinct. A business requires a tremendous amount of planning in order to be a success. So, take more time to think about important details. Also talk things over with an experienced, successful businessperson whom you can respect because of his or her high moral and ethical standards. Ask that person to help you think things through. Thinking of alternative courses of action and the consequences of compulsive behavior will greatly benefit your ability to deliver what's expected of you. If you're working on an important project, use enough self-control to stay focused until you've finished the task you have started. No one said it would be fun and games—but it's the right thing to do. And in the long run, there are rewards.

- As one who is impulsive, you'll be inclined to act first and think later. But sometimes this pattern of behavior can get you into trouble. Thinking through the consequences of an impulsive act may seem boring, but it may also keep you from making a serious mistake on the job.

- Avoid spontaneous career decisions without thinking through the long-term consequences. The grass always looks greener on the other side of the fence, but when you get there, the color seems to change. Without strong focus, you may be tempted to shift from one career endeavor to another. To a prospective employer this is interpreted as being just plain flaky.
- *Managers:* If you have a tendency to be impulsive, be careful not to confuse your employees by continually changing your mind about assignments. Keep your priorities clear. Then check to make sure that the employees stay on the prescribed course. This will increase productivity which, in turn, will make you look good to your superiors—and yourself!
- *Managers:* If you have a staff member under you who is impulsive, look for practical ways to help that person stay focused, especially in relating to important problems. That person's desire for immediacy may result in adopting premature decisions rather than considering enough options.
- *Managers:* If you are impulsive, your idea of a long conversation with an employee may be thirty seconds. Don't forget to spend time listening. This builds your employee's sense of dignity and self-worth. If you must limit a conversation, give valid reasons.

Deliberate. Are you known for carefully thinking things through? Do you avoid hasty decisions? Are you one who thinks twice before coming to a conclusion? Do you take time to carefully weigh the pros and cons before reaching a decision? Do you rarely make impulsive moves? If so, you are deliberate. You tend to be cautious, self-controlled, and consider the cause and effect of your actions. As a highly analytical person, accuracy is your forte! You approach most problems in a methodical manner and may require lots of time and information when making decisions. Your motto is, "I must know all the facts before I can make a valid decision." Hence, speed is your nemesis.

A deliberate person brings to the table the ability to view and consider the many sides of an issue. Acting with considerable restraint, decisions are carefully weighed and always have purpose.

The flip side to this personality trait is that a deliberate person may hesitate to take action when time is of the essence. The deliberate person's impulsive opposite will view him or her as inhibited, slow, and ineffective. Although a deliberate person may be partially motivated by fear of making a mistake, or from social hesitation, another major contributor to his or her deliberate style is the ability to suppress impulses. Accordingly, the deliberate person tends to make more rational decisions and avoid knee-jerk reactions. This trait is very helpful in occupations that call for great deliberation and care such as air traffic controllers and money managers.

The deliberate style involved is common among detail-oriented persons who prefer to review a considerable amount of information before making a decision. They deplore the idea of jumping to conclusions. For the deliberate person, pursuing topics in depth and delving into the intricacies of a situation are an enjoyable challenge.

People who are highly deliberative are often at their best when they are seen as a specialist or expert. They prefer closure rather than ambiguity and often have a need to be accurate. To do this, they hesitate to give their opinions until they have gathered enough information. Acquiring information is their way to avoid being caught off guard.

Good career paths for persons who fit this category are specialists in organizations rather than managers since managing consumes time that they would prefer using in analyzing data. A typical managerial lament: "I'm an engineer who got into management because it was the only path I could see to earn more money and more prestige. Now that I'm here, I feel frustrated and stressed because there just isn't enough time to do anything."

Tips for the Deliberate
- You might enjoy an occupation which capitalizes on your ability to be accurate. Typical jobs in this area might include basic accounting, proofreading, research, paralegal, engineering, project-oriented work, and middle management within a large organization.
- Teach yourself to make decisions without investing 100 percent

of your time and effort into the process of gathering information. Many times, you will be more effective if you set a time limit for making a decision. Remember, business requires not just thinking about a problem but taking action!

- If you work in a fast-paced environment, give the majority of your time to tasks that are of greatest significance, and spend less time and energy on those that are not as essential. Priority decisions can often be determined by whether a negative outcome could be disastrous or irreversible.

- Most career opportunities aren't equipped with iron-clad guarantees. If you are too cautious, you may move too slowly to take advantage of possible advances. There are times when going beyond your comfort zone in pursuing new plans and tackling new jobs can reap substantial rewards.

- *Managers:* Don't assume that a subordinate's decision is of poor quality just because he or she didn't spend a lot of time mulling over it. An impulsive employee who is also intelligent and experienced may make decisions or recommendations with lightning-bolt accuracy. What really matters is whether they are right, not how long it took them to form a conclusion.

- *Managers:* Spending too much time analyzing a situation can block you from actually moving ahead with your work. Guard against "analysis paralysis."

SUMMARY

The personality factors discussed in this chapter all relate to the broad personality trait of dependability, which, in the world of business, translates into how valuable you are to your employer. "Can I depend on you?" is the question your co-workers and bosses want to know.

Rule-keepers are more conscientious in their work because it's the right thing to do. But when it comes to rule-*breakers,* you can almost count on them to do their work *their* way rather than the way it was prescribed.

Those with an indirect or associative style of focus complete their work in a creative, dreamy style—if they can concentrate long enough to finish the job. On the other hand, persons with direct focus do what is immediately obvious, but they often overlook the big picture.

Orderly persons perform out of a need for exactness and demonstrate the fact that they meet their own, high personal ideals. The lax employee, however, will work when and if he or she feels like it—and lots of times the person doesn't.

Then there's the impulsive person who shoots from the hip, and depending on attributes such as experience, intelligence, and ability, may or may not hit the target. Lastly, the deliberate employee, while resisting impulsive action, offers accuracy, but not necessarily speed.

These dependability factors—or lack of them—contribute to your self-control, follow through, and overall ability to make things happen at work. They are important in determining how well you fit into the world of work!

5

The Way You See Reality

*Subfactors for Personality Pattern:
Emotional Sensitivity, Impulsiveness versus
Deliberation, Analytical Thinking*

Although the people you work with may dress appropriately, have a similar educational background, share fairly similar values, or even aspire to the same career goals, the way they think and make decisions can be space worlds apart. The contrast can be as striking as the difference between abstract art and high resolution photography.

The subject of how people see the same thing differently has been the topic of countless books and seminars as it relates to unlocking the secrets to successful relationships. The typical approach, for example, is to learn that women are one way, and men are another, so here is how you must adapt in order to have a peaceful coexistence.

The benefits that come from understanding the perceptual differences between your particular co-workers are immense. If you can figure out how your boss arrives at decisions, for example, you can probably determine the right approach to reach him or her. More importantly, being aware of your own style of perception and decision-making helps you to reinforce your strengths while compensating for your weaknesses. When the stakes are high, failing to guard against your perceptual weaknesses can cause the best-made plans to backfire.

Consider the case of a hard-nosed commercial real estate developer and his attorney who, while trying to reorganize an unprofitable investment, failed to consider the subjective elements of a decision and the consequences that would follow.

Nearly one thousand employees of a three-hundred-million-dollar resort gathered one afternoon in the grand ballroom for a special all-employee meeting. Although no one knew the purpose of the meeting, it was assumed that the employees would have a chance to meet the resort's owner and to hear about his plans for the future. Excitement was building as everyone realized how rare it was to assemble as one collective "family." Soon, however, the employees were to learn that the owner would not be present, but rather, was sending an attorney as his proxy.

Within a few minutes, the bustling of the crowd grew still and serious as the attorney coolly announced that the company was performing poorly and some major changes would soon be forthcoming. The attorney went on to say that half of the resort would be sold to a new owner. Several of the restaurants would be closed, numerous lay-offs could be expected, and that no one's job was secure! The crowd sat with open mouths, dazed eyes, pounding hearts, and absolute silence until one employee shouted, "Why is this happening to us? We've given the best years of our lives to this place." The attorney replied with sterile effect, "It's your fault. Obviously, *you* failed to make a profit."

In the months that followed the employees continued to talk about the day the owner and his "gun slinging" attorney "dropped the bomb." To make matters worse, a few evenings later, the television show, "Lifestyles of the Rich and Famous" happened to feature the resort's owner as he drove around town in his Rolls Royce. "Betrayal" became the rallying cry as word quickly spread among the employees. During the ensuing months, there were very few lay-offs. But morale had reached an all-time low none-the-less, and no one could put much heart in his or her work.

Company trust had been severed, and employees kept waiting for the "other shoe to drop."

"You look sad, what's wrong?" said a perplexed guest to a housekeeper who was obviously pouting while dusting the room. "We're not supposed to say, ma'am, but we've been treated something terrible by this hotel! Just something terrible!" replied the housekeeper. It goes without saying that the resort had lost its top-notch service rating. Soon, repeat business began to drop and word spread throughout the travel industry that it was best to avoid this facility because of all the in-house commotion. Hence, morale affected guest service, which, in turn, decreased profits—which was what the owner wanted to avoid.

It took the management team months to restore the damage that the owner and his hatchet man had effected in only a few minutes.

The owner, although a sharp businessman, lacked an awareness of relational dynamics. Communicating a message that essentially said, "You were the ones who blew it, so you're going to loose your jobs and we don't care what happens to you," was nothing short of shooting himself in the foot. He didn't understand the subjective side to decisions. Such perceptual "blind spots" made a bad situation much worse.

EMOTIONAL SENSITIVITY:
OBJECTIVE VERSUS SUBJECTIVE

The polarities of objective versus subjective experiences were first recognized by William James who dubbed them "tough-mindedness" and "tender-mindedness." The construct was further developed by psychologist Carl Jung who used the terms "thinker" versus "feeler."[1] Because of their inclusion in the popular Myers-Brigg Type Indicator instrument, I'm using the same terms. "Thinkers" make judgments based on logic, practicality, and hard-nosed evidence. "Feelers" are more self-indulgent and they experience a greater range and variety of emotions and inner experiences. Of course, "thinkers" can feel and "feelers" can think. Those who are in the middle of this continuum have the flexibility of using both modes of judgment. Most people, however, favor one style over another to some extent.

A caricature of these two contrasting styles can be seen in the television characters of Mr. Spock and Dr. McCoy from the original *Star Trek* television series. Viewers who remember Spock as the extremely logical Star Fleet science officer will get a sense of the quality of the highly objective thinker who was often criticized by Dr. McCoy for having no feelings. Dr. McCoy, on the other hand, was a feeler who was guided by compassion, repulsed by roughness, and easily offended by others who didn't share his emotional sensitivities.

"Thinkers." How about you? Are your thoughts realistic and tough-minded? Do you keep a cool head in a crisis? At work, do you have a hard-nosed, pragmatic attitude about what it takes to succeed? Do you keep turning conversations back to the original point? As a young person, were you exposed to the harsh realities of life at an early age? These are some of the decidedly businesslike characteristics of the cool, rational, objective thinker who holds everything to the litmus test of "the real world." Known for their rationality and self-reliance, objective thinkers are able to detach themselves from the emotional side of the equation in order to make realistic, often courageous decisions.

These rugged "John Wayne" types are often admired by co-workers who look up to them for their clear, no-nonsense reasoning. Thinkers value pragmatism and dislike generalities. What they relate to best are concepts that can be proven or in some way measured. "It has to make business sense" is their battle cry at work.

With their more limited range of feelings, objective thinkers can be color-blind to emotions. Sometimes they can become so emotionally detached from issues that they miss the hidden but vitally important interpersonal aspects. This can cause bad feeling in an office situation. As in the previous example of the resort owner, thinkers can be insensitive about "dropping the bomb" on employees, so the results often backfire.

Occupationally, objective thinkers rely more on facts than they do on feelings. For this reason, they seldom make good counselors or therapists. Rather, their nonsentimental, calculating, self-reliant approach makes them better suited for jobs that require swift decisiveness (fire fighting), directing people (police officers, plant supervisors), using machines or tools (mechanics), or dealing with hard scientific facts (engineers).

In the corporate world, their logical approach to problem-solving is well suited to activities like determining tasks, setting priorities, using resources, strategic planning, establishing budgets, and designing products. Thinkers often excel in upper corporate management where a heavy emphasis is placed on tying activity to bottom line profits. An executive committee, for example, without enough thinkers will have a difficult time making realistic, productive decisions. Thinkers who freely speak their minds may be hard-crusted to the point of cynicism, but in the long run their essential honesty will usually prove to be an asset.

A combination which spells trouble, however, is when a tough-minded thinker is also low on service and a rule-breaker. Occasionally, you'll find these persons in lower to middle management of large organizations. They're the ones who can hurt you and yet not feel your pain.

A few years ago I consulted with the executive management of a fitness complex which overlooked a beautiful lake and golf course. From the perspective of the club's members, it was a perfect place to unwind and relax. For employees, however, it was a dangerous place to work.

The manager of the club was a tough-minded lady who was noticeably lacking in interpersonal sensitivity. Her main objective was to turn a profit for the owners, even if it meant cutting a few corners in the safety of the operation.

I'll never forget the amazing story of one of the hourly employees whom I interviewed. After we had established some trust and rapport, she shared some aspects of her job that were troubling her. One of her duties was to wash and dry guest towels. The machines for this were situated outside the club house in a small patio that was adjacent to a golf course. Sometimes the golfers would hit balls off course and they would veer toward the spa patio and hit an attendant who would be loading clothes into the dryer. Upon being informed about the unsafe working conditions, the manager was unmoved. Instead of moving the machines or erecting a protective fence or wall, she found *football helmets* for the spa attendants to wear! Of course, this still left the rest of their bodies vulnerable to stray golf balls. This was but one example of the poor working conditions. No wonder employee turnover in the club house was out of control. Needless to say, that manager did not last very long.

Tips for Thinkers

- Most business problems involve subjective elements. If tuning in to your feelings is difficult for you, ask your co-workers for their input. Listen to their feedback without interruption and thank them for their honesty.
- Objective thinkers can be insensitive to the emotional needs of co-workers who are more subjectively oriented. If you must deal with people, think about more than just prioritizing work and meeting deadlines. When dealing with a co-worker, remember to make it a human and satisfying experience. And when you are in the position for giving feedback to a feeler, say something personal about what the other person did well.
- To show a feeler that you're listening and that you care, consider paraphrasing or repeating back what he or she has said, or share a similar experience of your own. The implicit message is, "I respect you and I'm listening because you are important."
- Don't expect others to be as logical and cool-headed as you. In fact, you may find it simply unbelievable that some people can be so indecisive or "stupid." When your co-workers irritate you, try to remember that their personalities are probably quite different from yours. You may get on their nerves as much as they do yours. On occasion be ready to ingest a big "tolerance pill."
- *Managers:* If you are a thinker, make it a point to emphasize the personal aspect of your *role* in the organization. "John, thanks for meeting with me. As you know, it's my job to come around to all the departments to make sure their forecasting is on target."
- *Managers:* If it's your job to supervise thinkers, you have a

responsibility to listen even though they may not be very assertive or forthright. In other words, make sure they have a chance to express their logic. Thinkers tend to see things in black and white terms and will feel frustrated if they aren't given a chance to express them.

"Feelers." Do you let your emotions rule your decisions? Are you inclined to be self-indulgent and soft? Are you empathetic toward the underdog? Do you seek reassurance and support from others? Do you consider yourself to be a "romantic"?

If so, you're a feeler. Feelers identify with others on an emotional level and see the world through idealistic and compassionate eyes. They are often sensitive, idealistic, fastidious, temperamental, and demanding.

The director of a singing group at a university gained a reputation among his students and colleagues for being a gifted and talented musician, but one who harbored personal eccentricities. Each year, for example, while taking this choral group on a singing tour the director would stop by a river bed and leave a message under a certain rock for others to find. According to a former student: "I called his office one day to say hello and ask him for some advice. Although I really didn't know him very well, out of the blue he verbally reprimanded me for sounding so cold and impersonal."

Feelers who are also introverted may have a difficult time expressing to others the intensity of their feelings. Often they gravitate toward work that offers a channel of expression for a feeling person. They may turn toward the arts and become involved in painting, music, or literary endeavors.

A feeler who is extroverted, however, has little difficulty expressing his or her feelings. A depth of compassion and sensitivity, combined with a desire to tell the world, often causes that person to be an outspoken proponent of what he or she feels is a worthy cause.

When working with others, feelers often place a high value on harmony and on the impact a decision will have on another person's feelings. I am reminded of two business persons that I know who are feeling and thinking opposites as well as assertive and nonassertive opposites. While visiting their offices on two separate occasions, I happened to have overheard them both as they responded to phone calls from stockbrokers who were making phone solicitations selling a so-called "incredible investment opportunity." The feeler, after listening to the sales pitch, politely explained, "We already have a stockbroker and our financial condition is such that we're really not able to do any investing right now, but thank you anyway for your call." At this point, the salesperson kept talking and the feeler eventually repeated the whole polite explanation.

The thinker, on the other hand, interrupted the sales person after just a few seconds of his pitch and asked, "Where are you calling from?" When he learned that the broker was out of state, he replied: "I only deal with brokers who are close enough for me to personally walk over to their offices and wring their necks should they have the misfortune of losing my money. Good bye."

Feelers are often found among the ranks of counselors, social workers, educators, political activists, clergy, psychologists, chefs, artists, musicians, nonprofit workers, and writers. They gravitate toward work requiring skill. Sometimes they may not function as well in a physically challenging occupation.

Tips for Feelers

- Feelers tend to disassociate themselves from objective facts, indulging in wishful thinking. Therefore, plan your obligations carefully and do not agree to complete a project unless you've had an opportunity to think through all the ramifications of your decision. Check with a thinker if there's any doubt as to the realism of your plans.
- Your information processing has to connect with feelings, and that can take time. Avoid jobs that require a lot of on-the-spot decisions. Prepare for meetings by listing important points that you would like to make. Be ready to answer questions relating to various facts and figures concerning your work.
- If your job requires teamwork and you work with a thinker, you can easily be misunderstood if you don't explain the logic behind your plans. Making decisions just because they feel right is not necessarily wrong, but make a point to translate your unspoken inclinations into logical points for your co-worker to digest.

- Make sure that you discover the individual work styles of each of your co-workers. When dealing with an objective thinker, remember that "actions speak louder than words." He or she will be much more impressed by what you do rather than what you say.

- *Managers:* Avoid giving feedback to a subordinate when you are in a bad mood and your feelings are strong. Employees are easily alienated when a manager is inconsistent in his or her moods. Instead, wait a few minutes and cool down, or even a few days, until you can make your comments on a more professional level.

- *Managers:* Most successful organizations have a bias toward task-oriented communication. The higher you move up the company ladder, the more you will need to convert your feeling-oriented comments into the language of logic, objectives, and reasoning.

Impulsiveness versus Deliberation. In the previous chapter the factor of impulsive versus deliberate thinking was discussed in light

---

The Distractability of Feelings

Feelers who are overly sensitive may have a hard time listening to what others are saying when they are distracted by their own feelings.

Before the introduction of a new computer system into the marketplace, the brilliant but demanding CEO insisted that the design manager lower the production cost of a special computer case from two hundred dollars to the impossible price of just fifteen dollars per unit. After weeks of berating the designers for their incompetence, it came out that the true cost of the case was indeed, two hundred dollars.

The same CEO, in searching for precisely the right shade of green for the company color, assigned a worker to search through thirty-seven color shades before finding what he wanted. According to an employee who was interviewed by Fortune magazine, "It was exasperating. The hardest thing was that I couldn't guess what was in his head. I wanted to say, 'Oh, come on. Green is green!'" Says a former executive who worked with this CEO: "Being around (him) is a reality distortion."[2]

of one's dependability. Let us briefly touch on this factor again since a person's ability to control impulses or feelings can greatly influence the amount of time he spends gathering data before deciding and taking action.

The impulsive person will want to spend very little time in the actual information-gathering process. The person would rather get on with the job of making up his or her mind. This approach is intuitive, rapid, and often based on trial and error. On the other hand, the person who deliberates wants to consider substantial amounts of information and needs extensive time to process his or her thoughts before making a decision.

The great trade-off between these two opposing styles is speed versus accuracy. In very general terms, managers and entrepreneurs are often called upon to make quick decisions, while those holding technical positions are functional specialists and require more precision and less risk. The implications for job-to-person match are obvious. Relations with co-workers are also influenced by this factor. For example, when impulsive and deliberate persons try to communicate with each other on a subject—like how much time should be spent in meetings and what depth and amount of information should be shared—there can be a wide variety of opinions. Greater detail on this potential problem is discussed in the final chapter where trait descriptions, illustrations, and tips are discussed in detail.

PROBLEM-SOLVER VERSUS REACTOR

Problem-solver. When planning projects do you think ahead? Do you consider a variety of choices and their consequences before making decisions? Are you generally able to reach your personal goals? Do you make a realistic assessment of what and when something must be accomplished? Do you see the hidden steps that are necessary in order to solve most problems? Do you cope well with frustrating situations? Do you ask pertinent questions? Do you adapt well to unexpected disappointments? If so, you're a problem-solver.

Problem-solvers face challenges in a timely manner using a lot of common sense. They think realistically about what they must do, both now and later, in order to achieve their goals or to overcome an obstacle. Problem-solvers set obtainable goals and do not try to do more than is possible. Problem-solvers are similar to thinkers in that they too, are logical. Thinkers act logically because they tune out emotions. Problem-solvers act logically because they understand the importance of both realistic thinking and the ability to continuously adapt to life's surprises. This kind of circumspection is extremely meaningful as it relates to a person's career and what one needs to do in order to get where he or she wants to be tomorrow.

Recently I had a discussion with a woman I'll call Sonya about some of her career interests. As we discussed her situation, I was impressed with how well she knew her personality strengths and motivations. She had already compiled a list of the things she wanted in a career. "I would like a job in the southern California area," Sonya said, "one that would capitalize on my ability to sell, persuade, and convince others as well as tap into my interest in relating to people on a personal basis. I would also like to use my talents and abilities benefiting others, while still helping a company make a profit. I would like an opportunity to advance to...." Sonya's level of planning was quite insightful—but not atypical of problem-solvers who like to think ahead.

In most situations, there are very few downsides to being a problem-solver. One exception, however, is when a person has a strong pattern of rule-breaking along with abilities for problem solving. This combination often describes an antisocial personality who breaks rules in an unusually cunning and smooth manner. These slippery characters are skilled in manipulation, wreak havoc and deception, and yet often evade arrest.

Anti-social personalities notwithstanding, the more of a problem-solver you are, the more resources you have to help you meet your personal and work-related goals. For this reason, it is generally considered a sign of good emotional health to be a problem-solver than its opposite, a reactor.

Tips for Problem-Solvers

- Your tendency to make good decisions and to tolerate frustration makes you well suited for a great variety of careers. Jobs that require both composure and responsibility are especially good fits for problem-solvers. These would include administrators, judges, police officers, pilots, school bus drivers, and certain jobs in the medical profession, to name only a few.

- Your decisive characteristics may prevent you from gaining the cooperation of your fellow employees. Allow time for them to see the problem clearly, discuss it, and then make a decision.

Reactor. Are you often overwhelmed by the challenges of the day? Have you had difficulty reaching your personal and career goals? Do you often make decisions without thinking of the consequences? Do small disappointments upset you greatly? If so, you're a reactor. Reactors are people who have a difficult time making realistic decisions, and tend to become easily frustrated when things don't go as planned. Lacking control over their emotions, reactors can also be moody and undependable. In emergencies or other crisis situations, reactors tend to "lose their cool." In making decisions, they often jump at what appears to be the first solution to a problem, which may not be the best.

Personality researcher Raymond Cattell, who called this style "affected by feelings," noticed that persons with this characteristic sometimes worked as accountants, clerks, farmers, artists, professors, writers, and employment counselors. Interestingly, Cattell also discovered that those who are "affected by feelings" were frequently raised in matriarchal families where a strong relationship with a father figure was missing.[3]

If you are a reactor, don't immediately despair. A great number of reactors do very well both in their career and personal lives. However, if you frequently feel frustrated over things, or if you have problems relating with people, or with judgment, consider getting professional help.

Tips for Reactors

- Try to avoid occupations that require you to deal with stressful situations or emergencies. Methodical work that doesn't have very many ups and downs would be a better match for you.

- Recognize your tendency to make unrealistic decisions. Before acting on a matter, weigh the pros and cons more carefully and consider the consequences to your intended actions. If a decision is important, ask a friend to help you think through the ramifications of various alternatives. Your friend will be glad to give his or her opinions, and you will benefit from talking the matter over.
- To avoid frustrating situations, plan ahead. Guard against leaping into a task solely on instinct.
- *Managers:* If you're a reactor, guard against your tendency to be easily upset or moody. Displaying inconsistent or inappropriate emotions builds a wall between you and the people whose loyalty you need.
- *Managers:* Beware of situations where you must make a hurried decision in an area that is new to you. Your best decisions come about in areas where you are already experience or knowledgeable. Make a point to be "up to speed" before you allow yourself to be put on the spot in a new area.

SUMMARY

Whether you're making a three-hundred-million-dollar decision or just trying to figure out how to spend the rest of your day, your degree of emotionality, deliberateness, and ability to problem-solve colors your perception of the world. Thinkers are tough-minded and tend to see the bottom line. Feelers rely on their emotional reactions for direction. Deliberators like to digest substantial information, while impulsive persons experience a rapid succession of ideas but spend a lot less time on each one of them. Problem-solvers think realistically and are cool under pressure. Reactors feel the heat as they try to adapt to the demands of everyday life.

Have you discovered yourself or the people where you work in any of these personality descriptions?

6

Do You Fit In?

Subfactors: Dependence, Assertiveness, Orientation to Change, Trust, Risk, Rule Conformity, Self-Concept Variant Pattern: Autonomy Versus Structure.

THE MEN THAT DON'T FIT IN

There is a race of men who don't fit in,
A race who can't stay still;
So they break the hearts of kith and kin,
And they roam the world at will.
They range the field, and they rove the flood;
And they climb the mountain's crest;
Theirs is the curse of the gypsy blood,
And they don't know how to rest.
If they just went straight they might go far,
They are strong and brave and true,
But they are always tired of the things that are,
And they want the strange and new....
He's a rolling stone, and it's bred in the bone;
He's a man who won't fit in.

Robert W. Service
Songs of a Sourdough[1]

"**Y**OU CAN ONLY HAVE SO MANY LEADERS in a large organization," said Neil, as he reflected on why he left a cushy job with a Fortune 500 corporation. "What they mostly want are lunch pail Joes who will follow the program—people who will do what they're told, follow procedures, put their shoulder behind the stone and push! They're not looking for leaders, just followers. I was a division-level corporate manager, and I couldn't take the pressure of them telling me *not* to tell the truth. If they were losing money or if there was a better way of doing something, I told them. But when you're the truth-bearer, you make enemies and then there are fewer and fewer places in the corporation where you cán go. I finally left to start my own business. After being away for seventeen years, I'd never go back."

Robert, on the other hand, is a CPA with a medium-sized firm. "At my firm there's plenty of long hours, but they don't push you as much as the 'Big 6' accounting firms. At first, management scrutinizes your performance and makes it clear what's expected of you. Eventually they don't check on you as much. I've been with the firm ever since I got out of college, and I basically like the setup. I enjoy most of my assignments except for dealing with a few organizations which are a mess financially. The support staff that I have is pretty friendly; that makes a difference too. I don't know if I would want to be a junior partner. It's a lot of stress."

Neil functions best independently. Robert prefers moderate structure. It would be a mistake for them to switch jobs.

Within organizational life, one's autonomy is related to how much independent thinking and decision-making a job allows one to exercise. A small business owner, for example, enjoys extensive freedom. Increasing government regulations are his or her nemesis. On the other hand, a clerical worker in a bureaucratic organization will be saddled by a massive number of rules—usually set by a far-away decision-maker.

The concept of autonomy versus structure relates to a person's sense of separateness from others. One's degree of separateness of feelings and thoughts create a boundary that is similar to a property line. The autonomous person has very clear "no trespassing" signs and will throw people off the property who are not welcome. The person who desires structure, however, wants people to come on the property and set up camp. This "occupation" creates a lack of independent thinking and invites other people to take control. A highly autonomous person, however, not only desires separateness but also functions independently. Neil, for example, eventually started his own business, so he wouldn't have to do what other people expected of him.

The personality factors which relate to the pattern of autonomy versus structure are numerous and are drawn from subfactors found among the patterns of people orientation, extroversion, power, and dependability. In particular, an autonomous person may be assertive (wanting one's own way), change oriented (not fitting with the status quo), low on trust (suspicious of others' decisions), high in self-confidence (belief in one's own choices), low on dependence (finding sufficiency in oneself), high on risk-taking (venturing out on one's own), and a rule-breaker (not conforming to the expectations of others).

When several of these traits are found in one person, you will see an individual who values extensive personal freedom in establishing his or her own boundaries on the job. This translates to such things as setting one's own objectives, setting one's work hours, and having control over resources.

The opposite of each of the above traits would relate to a person who desires a great deal of structure. These subfactors would include low assertiveness (acquiescence to others), traditionalism (clinging to old ideas), high trust (accepting others' decisions), low self-confidence (needing support from others), high dependence (drawing resources outside oneself), low risk-taking (playing it safe), and rule-keeping (conforming to the expectations of others). A combination of several of these traits describe persons who want to submit to the boundaries that other people set. At work, this includes a desire to know what expectations and limits an employer or boss has, along with a desire for substantial feedback to gauge their compliance with the rules. Such people like to play it safe.

This chapter is organized differently from the other personality chapters. This is because the numerous subfactors which contribute to the pattern of autonomy versus structure have already been described and discussed in previous chapters. Therefore, I will limit the present discussion to the application of the pattern as a whole to the workplace environment.

AUTONOMY PATTERN

Do you enjoy your own company as much or more as being with others? Are you very confident about making your own decisions? Do you hold fast to your positions even when you're with others who disagree? Do you place a high value on your privacy and freedom? Are you aggressive, even a bit daring? Do you prefer to take your own initiative rather than follow other people's structure? Do you tend to distrust what other people say? If so, you're probably an independent person with a high need for autonomy. The following are some general guidelines for independent, autonomous persons.

Tips for Highly Autonomous Persons

- Your autonomy is high. Can you work in a structured or routine work setting? Consider a job that gives you enough leeway in your day-to-day decisions because you don't need much supervision. Although some large organizations have such positions, small firms often have fewer restrictions. If you don't mind low job security, you might consider being an entrepreneur so you can be your own boss.
- Because you prefer to make your own decisions, others may see you as unwilling to take advice, or worse, peg you as a loose cannon. If your superior feels that you are unwilling to listen or accept guidance, this could have an adverse affect on your performance ratings. Your boss wants to know that you are open to input and receptive to advice. Guard your reputation by finding out what your boundaries are before you cross the line.
- You may have a difficult time trusting other people's ideas. Learn

to accept the judgment of others and use their ideas. You simply do not have the time to research all of the answers yourself. Conversely, don't over-delegate. Autonomous people often expect others to think as independently and self-sufficiently as they do.

- You're likely to be very task-focused at work. Take the time to pay more attention to social nuances. You can't be a complete lone ranger and get ahead in most organizations. Pay attention to the feelings of others. Show an interest in what other people are doing. Join groups and be friendly. Find common interests and experiences with your co-workers. Stay in contact and culti-vate relationships if you want to advance your career.

- *Managers:* Since you tend to be quite self-sufficient, your em-ployees may suspect that you think of them as "cry babies" when they bring concerns to you. Make sure to tell that person how important his or her contribution is to your department.

- *Managers who supervise autonomous employees:* Independent employees need freedom. Give them your basic expectations, set limits, and explain consequences. Then let them devise their own way to get the work done. If they cannot produce, then you may need to assert more structure.

STRUCTURE PATTERN

Are you a rather polite person? Do you lean on others to help you make decisions? Do you shy away from taking risks? Do you often look toward others for advice? Do you sometimes question your own ability to make decisions? Are you traditional in your thinking? Do you normally believe what others say? Do you try to do what others would consider the appropriate thing to do? If so, you have a preference for support and structure.

Persons with this pattern generally have low-key, dependent, unassuming, and somewhat passive personalities.

At work, they usually arrive at decisions with the help of others. A good work fit is often in well-defined, structured organizations or work units that stress participative decision-making. If you enjoy structure, you're probably more comfortable working with a team or under direct supervision rather than venturing out on your own. The policies and clearly prescribed work roles of a large organization will provide you with the feeling of security and stability that you desire (although very few large organizations can actually offer job security in today's environment). Military life would be an example of a work environment where almost every aspect of a job is regulated and scheduled.

Tips for Persons Who Prefer Structure

- Find a job that has considerable structure and social contact. Large organizations, for example, often provide a lot of direction. You may prefer a supervisor who clearly defines his or her expectations and priorities. In addition, make sure you have a job that offers enough social contact. You may do well in a group project environment.
- You may have difficulty working in a setting that requires a great deal of independence. Guard against leaning on your co-workers or boss to make decisions for you. Otherwise, people will see you as a clinging vine. In the business world, managers often reward employees who dare to take initiative. So learn to trust your own judgment.
- Perhaps your interest in seeking other people's advice is rooted in a lack of self-confidence. You may actually think of yourself as unable to make good decisions. Learn to trust yourself. Let your confidence show. Talk about those things that you know something about. Don't simply play the role of spectator in conversations.
- When making decisions, make sure that you don't give in to social pressure from your work group. Remember that one thousand Frenchmen *can* be wrong! Don't compromise your honest opinions when your boss asks for them. Your honesty can gain his or her respect and your directness will look less superficial.
- If open disagreement is difficult for you, therapy, assertiveness training, or a support group may be of great benefit to you. In

business, avoiding unpleasant situations doesn't make problems go away—it only postpones them and makes you less effective. Learn to deal with problems head on.

- *Managers:* If you prefer structure, make sure that you do not stifle employees who are less rigid than you. Give your subordinates basic boundaries and expectations of what you want them to accomplish. Then let them do their work.
- *Managers who supervise employees who prefer structure:* Make sure that your priorities and other expectations are clear with these employees. Substantial time will be required by you to encourage them.

SUMMARY

The more one accommodates a work role to meet a person's preference for either structure or autonomy, the more work becomes a win-win situation. For the structured individual, knowing the other person's expectations and limits are reassuring. For the autonomous person, freedom is a huge contributor to work satisfaction. If your job is a poor fit in these areas, maybe it's time to transfer to another department or possibly seek other employment.

7

The Creative Juices—
How Your Ideas Flow

*Subfactors: Focus, Orientation to Change,
Experiential Style, Complexity*

FIFTY YEARS AGO who would have thought that a talking mouse would be the dominating force behind a multi-billion dollar empire? It took a person like Walt Disney who was not only a dreamer but also a driver to inspire and push others to follow his vision of a family theme park based on cartoon characters. Walt Disney is part of history, not only because of his ability to generate creative ideas, but because he could light fires under people that made them produce.

"I would see people coming and going down the hallways," said a Disney friend and former co-worker, "and you just knew that Walt was getting the most out of each and every one of them."[1]

"Do you want to go to lunch?" said one animation artist to another.

"No, I have a Walt Disney stomach today."

Creativity is not just limited to rare human beings like Walt Disney; businesses and corporations all across America are full of creative people. Many of them, however, go unappreciated or unrewarded. In the corporate world, for example, the security of duplicating what has worked in the past often rates a higher priority than trying something new and innovative. As Yogi Berra's much quoted phrase puts it, "If it ain't broke, don't fix it." This tendency of not adapting is why many flourishing businesses of yesterday are now mere memories. It takes courage to move in the direction of new, untried areas, but many times it's the only way for a company to survive in today's fast-paced, high-tech marketplace.

One organization with a tradition of promoting creativity and risk taking, however, is 3M. Their policy which permitted technical personnel to spend 15 percent of their time at work on personal ideas for the company helped Art Fry invent Post-It Notes™. According to 3M, Fry came up with the idea for Post-It Notes while singing in his church choir. He wanted a bookmark that wouldn't fall out of his hymnal but could be removed when no longer needed. Fry remembered a so-called "superglue" that a colleague had developed, and that it didn't stick very well. Fry hurried back to the lab and nine months later had perfected Post-It Notes, the small yellow memo pads that press on and peel off such items as books, computers, refrigerators, and telephones.

For 3M, it became a multi-million-dollar money maker. It fits with their goal to derive 25 percent of each year's sales from products that didn't exist five years earlier. For Fry, it was just another extension of his personality. As a young person, Fry had the same knack for invention. He would turn a pile of boards into a toboggan for use in the winter, and then change it into a shack in the summer. Fry, when speaking about the success of Post-It Notes says, "It's like watching your kids grow up and do well in the world."

How creative are you? Does your job stir your creativity and challenge your mind? Many of today's jobs are designed more for compliance than for creative thinking or decision-making. Even positions with great sounding titles are often quite routine and boring. Creativity, by itself, is a way of originating thoughts. What you do with those thoughts, however, depends on other personality factors such as self-control and assertiveness.

FOCUS: DIRECT VERSUS INDIRECT

The focus factor contributes to the personality characteristics of both dependability and creativity. If you have a direct focus, it's easier to be dependable. If your focus is indirect, you have a creative advantage. Since the focus factor has already been described in chapter four, "Can We Depend On You?", my reference to focus here will only be as it relates to creative thought processes rather than dependability.

The distinction between direct and indirect focus might be illustrated by a person who walks down a flight of stairs. One person with strong direct focus would probably be aware of each and every step. Conversely, the person with indirect focus would most likely be thinking of other things that are completely unrelated to what's happening in the present. It is the disregard of immediate surroundings that enables those tuned in to indirect focus to think of a hundred other things at once. The downside to this pattern of highly associative thinking is, of course, that indirect or "unfocused" people find it difficult to keep organized and be dependable. There's too much racing in one's thinking at the same time. The benefit for creative thought, however, is enormous.

Indirect Focus. Immersed in a world of intriguing inner thought, a person with strong indirect focus pays little attention to the obvious present. Rather, he or she daydreams, and free-associates, relying on memories, ideas, and mental images. This "absentminded" style has been shown to be the cause of frequent accidents as indirect focused people tend to ignore their immediate senses. But this style can also be the wellspring for the abundance of original ideas.

John, an independent consultant, was in a hurry to find a nine-by-twelve envelope because he had promised to mail a report to a friend and the postman would be arriving in ten minutes. "Otherwise I'm going to have to call Federal Express," thought John, "and that's more money than I want to spend." Realizing his absent-mindedness, John started looking around the office to see if maybe he could find an envelope hidden underneath a pile of papers somewhere. Of course, each pile that he looked through reminded him of an idea and soon his thoughts were splintering off into dozens of additional directions. Under one of the piles was an unused Federal Express overnight pack. This was the impetus for John's solution.

Gazing at the blue and red plastic Federal Express envelope, John noticed that it couldn't be used for regular mail because it had their bold logo on the outside. But John looked beyond the immediately obvious. Without hesitation, he put his hand inside the envelope and turned it inside out. Now it was a large, white envelope—just what he had been looking for. His contents went inside the envelope and the inside-out flap was doubled over twice and taped. Incidentally, John doesn't recommend that you do the same.

All day and all night, this type of thinking is second nature for people like John who link together ideas that to others would be unconnected. Unfortunately, such creativity is not always encouraged by organizations. Most businesses reward following rules more than generating new ideas. Because people with indirect focus often pay little attention to external details, but tend to have an internal focus, they are often misunderstood by their co-workers who consider them to be either "scatterbrained" or lazy. For this reason, some will receive poor performance ratings. If this rejection by co-workers persists, internally focused persons can become depressed, alienated, or retreat into their own inner world or even begin to suffer from an addiction.

Tips for Those with Indirect Focus

- Choose a career that will allow you to use your vivid imagination and innovative ideas. Certain jobs in entertainment, academia, the arts, sciences, marketing, engineering, writing, editorial planning, and architecture are examples of possible good fits.
- Your less creative but more practical work associates are likely to reject you unless you train yourself to pay attention to details that are important to your job. Gain a reputation for producing quality work.

- *Managers:* If you are creative, try to delegate the routine jobs to others who seem to thrive on detail-oriented tasks. Focus on utilizing your time and energies through your treasury of unique ideas.

Note: more tips for this factor are listed under chapter four as they relate to dependability.

Direct Focus. People who pay close attention to their obvious, immediate surroundings tend to favor a style of external, or direct focus. They form ideas by using their five senses rather than a free floating world of ideas. They prefer familiar, predictable, and proven ways of doing things. Unconventional ideas would often be considered eccentric by those who have direct focus. At work they're usually on time, reliable, and pay close attention to the events that surround them. In many occupations, this trait goes beyond being an asset; it is essential. When traveling as an airline passenger, for example, no one wants an absent-minded pilot or a pilot who experiments by trying out new routes! The field of law enforcement is another example of a good occupational fit for persons with direct focus.

A few years ago I had the opportunity to spend two days with the Narcotics Interceptor Squad of the Miami Police Department, also known as "Miami Vice." These brave men and women risk their lives each day as they track down drug dealers and catch them in the act of selling "crack" cocaine. One evening, the squad was conducting a "reverse sting" operation. This tactic entailed arresting several "crack" dealers along a particular city block and, in their place, susbstituting police officers who masqueraded as the original drug dealers! Customers, as they would drive home from work, would come to a certain street looking for the "crack" dealers who usually "hung out" there. After buying some drugs from an undercover officer, the offenders would not be arrested until they were a several blocks away from the reverse sting area. After all, why give away the element of surprise?

For both the decoy officers and the arresting "take down" officers, the process involved constant observation and description of suspect behavior. Dress, demeanor, and transportation all had to be mentally noted with painstaking accuracy. The decoys and the arresting officers had developed amazing powers of observation. In one instance, a suspect fled arrest and the sergeant I was riding with gave detailed descriptions over his car radio of everything that was happening while driving his squad car at forty miles per hour in reverse!

Like these police officers, persons with direct focus pay more attention to their immediate surroundings than their inner associations, and their rate of accidents is much lower than more absent-minded persons. They have great memories, too. In terms of creativity, however, a person with direct focus will generate fewer ideas than his absent-minded counterpart because he's paying attention to the immediate rather than dreaming.

Tips for Persons with Direct Focus

- You're better at conventional work which requires following policies and procedures than you are at originating new ideas or gaining insights. Don't get in over your head at a job that constantly requires you to think innovatively. Your strong suit is your keen alertness. Occupationally, mechanical or procedural jobs may be a better fit for you. These include such positions as bank managers, plant supervisors, engineers, mechanics, fire fighters, flight attendants, geologists, electricians, and police officers, to name a few.

- Other people may see you as predictable or one-dimensional. Learn to think beyond the obvious facts that you observe. Seeing the big picture means going beyond the "how" questions to thinking theoretically about the "why."

- *Managers:* If you tend to view things with a direct focus, be willing to think through a problem from several perspectives. The hunches and ideas of your employees, especially those who are by nature quite creative, can be very valuable to you. Be careful not to stifle the creativity of your subordinates.

- *Managers:* Learning to think more creatively and progressively can help you advance to higher levels within your organization. To help expand your thinking, consider taking a course or two on creativity or visionary management.

Note: More tips for this factor are listed in chapter four as they relate to the dependability pattern.

ORIENTATION TO CHANGE:
INNOVATORS VERSUS TRADITIONALISTS

In a previous chapter on power needs, the orientation to change factor was discussed in relation to the "radical" person who rejects tradition and resists being told what to think or do. In this chapter, I will limit my discussion to the change factor as it relates to the pattern of creative thinking.

"They're a bunch of idiots," criticized Walter, "they don't know what they're doing, and it's scary because the people at the head office are deciding on things they know nothing about." Walter is the creator of an innovative computer program that the "head office" distributes. In his sixties now, Walter has held a variety of jobs with some very prestigious companies—but stayed with none of them very long. At each corporation or government agency where Walter has worked, there inevitably came a time when he would butt heads with an "imbecile" and then leave for greener pastures. Although Walter is generally very pleasant, when he and I last spoke, I could tell that he was upset. He mentioned that his software distributor had turned down a new product idea that he hoped they would carry.

Walter is an example of a creative person whose personality is so change-oriented that he seems radical at times. Everywhere Walter has worked, his innovative ideas have been so ahead of his time that they would eventually fall upon deaf ears. This frustration, which innovators feel when they face rejection, drove him to the point of starting his own business.

Innovators. Do you find yourself intolerant of the status quo? Are your thoughts ahead of your time? Do you easily detach yourself from situations that you find to be unrewarding? Do you think about the future more than you do the past?

If so, you are an innovative thinker, a creator of new ideas. Some innovators have come from home situations where there has been considerable conflict with an authority figure. As a result, these innovators are inclined to question, analyze, and confront conventional ideas. If you are an innovator, you're more creative than the average person. You may do well in the arts and sciences, or as an independent, self-employed person.

Take the case of Bill Gates, the billionaire Harvard dropout and CEO of Microsoft, which is one of the most successful start-up companies in American history. According to James Wallace of the Seattle Post, Gates was a very bored student at Harvard and rarely attended classes. Instead, Gates could usually be found playing poker or spending time in the computer lab. As a businessman, he developed a reputation for ruthlessness, even if it meant backing out on deals. He made enemies. Nevertheless, he is one of the wealthiest men in America—to the tune of about seven billion dollars and a corporate staff of thirteen thousand, many of whom are millionaires. According to Wallace, Gates can be quite critical of the ideas of others, saying things like, "That's the stupidest software that's ever been written" (talk show interview on KKLA, June 15, 1993). Although not all innovators are ruthless or caustic, many of them are impatient and quite critical of others.

Tips for Innovators

- Make sure your job allows you opportunities to innovate and experiment because you'll be inclined to question almost everything that other people do at work. A smaller organization in a growth mode that is known for its progressiveness, for example, would be a better fit for you than most large, more bureaucratic organizations.

- Innovators are often intolerant of "tried and true" ways of thinking. If you're frustrated by bureaucracy and restrictions, consider working for a smaller organization or becoming self-employed. Within any organization, however, seek a role that allows you the greatest amount of freedom and decision-making relative to your field of expertise.

- Highly innovative persons often find it hard to deal with authority or to compromise with others. For this reason, they often receive negative performance ratings from supervisors since they are seen as insubordinate. Make sure that you establish harmonious working relations with your boss. From time to time this may mean taking a "tolerance" pill when others seem too myopic and don't share your farsightedness.

- Innovators usually make friends and contacts with others who think in a like-minded manner. In time, you may limit yourself to a social group that thinks quite similarly. Having friends who are so alike can cause you to narrow your perspective. Strive for a mix of friends and work associates with a variety of views to stay fresh and well rounded.

- *Managers:* If you're an innovator, you'll probably want your organization to make some changes. Success in implementing organizational change begins with paying close attention to the needs of your employees and being sensitive to company tradition before setting out to revise the whole company structure. For example, if your ideas were implemented, what would others in the organization stand to gain or lose? If others fear your ideas, it is best to introduce changes in small, nonthreatening doses before taking larger steps. Be patient, change is a process that is often best implemented over time.

Note: More tips for this factor are listed under chapter three as they relate to the power pattern.

Traditionalists. People who think in a more traditional manner enjoy the familiar and are often slow to change. Their outlook predisposes them to place confidence in the "truth" that they were taught as children. Because of this they respect authority and honor tradition. Traditionalists look for dependable work and strive to be dependable employees. Bosses and co-workers usually appreciate them for their faithful and dutiful attitude toward their job. What traditionalists find stressful, however, is dealing with change. Because traditionalists place confidence in existing ideas and structures, they tend to embrace change slowly. Their preference is to hold on to the past.

Mary, for example, put off learning how to use a computer for the better part of ten years. When she finally did, it was at the prodding of her boss. Once the edict came down that she must "learn or be lame," she began to dread the frustrating experience of needing to learn a complicated process. When she had actually completed the computer course, however, she was glad she had done it. It wasn't long, however, before Mary realized that a new, updated version of the computer program had arrived at the office and she would soon be expected to learn that too. Her sense of dread came over her again. Then, after that, of course, came the new phone system. Mary was in a dither.

Tips for Traditionalists

- In the right organization, your preference for following established ways of doing things will be viewed as loyal and desirable service. Banking, manufacturing, mechanics, or farming, for example, are typical occupations geared to reward those who follow prescribed methods of operation.

- Because you rely more on ideas and memories from the past, you may not have an opinion on something that catches you off guard other than to look back to see what's been done before. So learn to brainstorm. If your job calls for originality, you may be able to lean on a co-worker who is quite different from yourself in this area. When you're away from this person's influence, however, you're back to square one. Take seminars on increasing your creative thinking. Learn to think of possibilities!

- *Managers:* Be careful that you don't limit the creativity of others whose thinking is more original than yours. Guard against saying, "No, that won't work. We've tried it once before about ten years ago." Or, "No that won't work because we've never tried that before." Your tendency will be to wait too long to implement a change.

- *Managers:* If you are a traditionalist, your views may be reassuring to others in your organization who share them, but guard against accepting people just because they are likeminded. Every executive team or strategic planning unit should have one or two "pot stirrers" in order to infuse group decision-making with fresh thinking.

- *Managers:* Because of your rather traditional way of thinking, you may feel quite comfortable with long-standing rules and restrictions. In most work settings, too many rules can stymie hands-on involvement and reduce personal responsibility. Give people basic boundaries and expectations and then reward their superior performance.

Note: More tips for this factor are listed under chapter three as they relate to the power pattern.

EXPERIENTIAL STYLE: OPEN VERSUS CLOSED

A researcher by the name of Douglas Bray conducted a long-term study of AT&T employees who had just graduated from college. Specifically, he compared the career progression of those who majored in the humanities and social sciences with those who majored in business and engineering. At the outset of their careers, the liberal arts group was identified by managers as having higher potential than its narrower, more specialized counterpart. After twenty years with the company, 43 percent of the humanities and social science majors had risen to middle and higher levels of management, while only 23 percent of engineers and 32 percent of business majors had performed as well.[2]

This study, and others like it, suggest that students who are able to broaden their focus beyond solely a technical or specialty area will move ahead of those with a narrower, more closed educational background. One need not have a liberal arts education, however, to be able to think broadly or have a wide range of interests. Open thinking is, in part, a personality factor.

I've included it in the creativity chapter because, as you will shortly see, one's degree of openness to new experiences, ideas, and feelings relates to creative thinking. An open experiential style is marked by a person's aesthetic sensitivity, enjoyment of variety, intellectual curiosity, and discovery of inner sensitivities.

"Open" people are curious about life, seeking to discover new things about areas with which they're not familiar. They are interested in lifelong learning and often react with great intensity to art, music, literature, history, or travel. They seek out new ways to look at problems and want to know about other people's ideas—even if they're in opposition to their own. To this end they earnestly try to understand and even remember information that disagrees with their views. "Open" persons often have an imagination which helps produce expanded awareness and creative thinking.

Persons who are more "closed" have a narrower range of interests, pursuing new ideas with less vigor and intensity. In their work experience they often need less change and variety than their "open" counterparts. In terms of ideas, familiar notions are preferred and they dislike information that is contrary to what they presently believe. Being closed to experience does not necessarily imply an authoritarian personality or lower intelligence. It does relate to being less interested in experiencing new ideas and feelings.

Openness. Are you deeply interested by music, art, history, literature, or nature? Do you pay attention to those whose ideas are different than yours? Are you an adventurous, curious type of person? Are your interests deep and varied? Do you have frequent intellectual discussions? If so, you lean toward openness. Your style indicates that you are a curious, inquiring person who is influenced by a wide range of experiences, thoughts, and emotions.

"Open" persons love learning new things and usually have a strong desire to increase their understanding of the world. The open person will also value his or her own emotional reactions to a variety of experiences just so they may be experienced. Ralph von Williams once wrote a song entitled, "Let Beauty Awake for Beauty's Sake." This type of strong appreciation for aesthetic beauty is often an important part of the open person's value system.

The open person's thirst for new and different feelings and experiences is sometimes demonstrated by a high level of intellectual curiosity. Openness is not necessarily related to intelligence. Some very intelligent people are quite closed to new experiences. In addition, some very open people are quite limited in intellectual capacity.

Occupationally, open persons may move from one field to another, but they always bring their insights and experiences with them wherever they go. I am reminded of Jan, a communications and drama professor with a private college. When she's not teaching or directing, she likes to attend a variety of productions from both American and European playwrights. Jan likes to travel abroad and she especially likes to stay in people's homes rather than a "plain vanilla" hotel.

Seymour is a writer and public speaker. His stock and trade are the world of ideas. Whenever he has a chance, even if he is on the road, Seymour loves to go to the best bookstore in town to peruse magazines and all the new books and commentaries. Seymour looks for local, national, and international trends.

Pat is an elementary school teacher from the midwest. During the school year she looks for opportunities to pick up new ideas at teaching conferences. During the summer months, Pat takes various courses at universities in addition to traveling overseas. Whether Pat is visiting Europe or Hawaii, she always wants to learn about the local culture. Having traveled with Pat on a tour, I remember occasions when she would buy books, tapes, and clothes to take home to her "kids." Known for being an innovative educator, it wasn't long before she caught the attention of her principal as well as the district superintendent. In time, she was invited to join the central staff as director of curriculum for the entire school district. In looking back over her career, Pat has had a marvelous experience as an educator. The boys and girls of her district have also benefited from her open style.

Tips for Those with an Open Style

- Seek out organizations and roles that will tap into your open style. Celebrate your creative ideas, skills, and wide-ranging personal experiences in a work role that matches your open style. Creative opportunities are often found among the ranks of higher education, the arts, music, writing, speaking, teaching, research, ministerial work, political science, and biology—to name just a few.

- Although you naturally have many interests, once you've acquired a broad education, learn to focus your energies on those things that will help your career. What new knowledge, skills, or training can you acquire to keep yourself marketable in today's changing and unstable job market? Is the area where you would like to expand too narrow? Will it offer new opportunities five years from now?

Closed. Was the game of "make-believe" uninteresting to you as a child? Does poetry and music have a limited effect on you? Do you experience strong feelings quite rarely? Do you prefer familiar surroundings over new places? Do you try to avoid discussing ideas with someone who will disagree with your viewpoint? Do you enjoy working at a routine job that doesn't vary much from day to day?

If so, your experiential style is more closed than open. You probably enjoy a fixed routine more than change and are less tempted to investigate possibilities that new ideas present. You're loyal to those familiar things in your life and have less desire to seek out or explore new interests or experiences than your "open" opposites. In addition, you are less apt to be moved by music, art, poetry, literature, or nature. Your work may involve a technical or functional specialty.

Occupationally you will find that your style is well suited for a large number of jobs. Because most organizations break work up into "bite-sized" pieces, the majority of available jobs center around following directions rather than being open to new ideas. This is particularly true for entry level and lower management positions where the largest number of jobs are found.

Working to involve the "rank and file" in decisions and tapping into their world of experience and creativity is a popular topic at business schools and conferences, but employee involvement has not been widely implemented into industry. If you would like to expand your career beyond entry level or lower management, however, you should begin by expanding yourself beyond the confines of your present thoughts and skills.

Tips for Those with a Closed Style

- Guard against getting stuck in any one way of thinking. You may be quite proficient in your functional area, yet lack the benefits of a broader, more versatile understanding. Your limited exposure to the "liberal arts" can decrease your reservoir of new ideas from which to draw.
- Being closed to experience can make you seem uninteresting to

your supervisors. This can negatively impact your ability to make a good first impression. At work, try to put some color and variety into your meetings and discussions, even though that may feel uncomfortable.

- Consider taking up a hobby. New activities after work will introduce some variety into your life and reduce your chances for burnout and possibly provide a healthier and fresher attitude toward your work as well.

- The ability to discuss a wide variety of topics will make you a more interesting person to the people in management. Try to keep up with news, business trends, social issues, and scientific development.

- *Managers:* If you are a closed person, your ability to focus on current everyday objectives is admirable. Remaining closed to new ideas, however, may keep you from considering important changes. Don't get left behind.

- *Managers:* If you find that you must supervise closed persons, work toward broadening their understanding of their work unit, perhaps by implementing some type of job rotation. For example, ask a salesperson to spend a day with customer service or vice versa. Another approach would be to assign a "closed" employee to a cross-functional work team where he or she could expand in thinking and problem-solving.

INFORMATION PROCESSING: CONCRETE VERSUS COMPLEX

Jack is a research scientist who applies all his creative and intellectual energies toward trying to solve the pollution problem. His summer job with NASA entails conducting scientific experiments while riding on airplanes. The purpose of this procedure is to study the level of ozone depletion, and hopefully determine its cause. This winter Jack will be on an ice cap in Siberia running large drills to secure a core of ice for a special study. The levels of pollution in the ice are analyzed and related to incidents which have occurred in the past. When not working for NASA, he teaches university courses in New England.

As a child in school, Jack could divide and multiply before he knew what the concepts meant. Just give him the numbers and boom—he would know the answers without even knowing why. Jack's high IQ combined with a Ph.D. in geology from a top university make him well-suited to face the challenges of his very complex job. He is able to understand extremely advanced principles of math and science, to consider alternatives with their interactions, and to produce some valuable research. Jack thrives on acutely complex problems and is one of the leading experts in his field.

Incidentally, Jack is a gourmet chef, wears his hair in a pigtail, and doesn't own a pair of shoes other than boots and Birkenstocks™. Jack is an example of someone who is both intellectually gifted as well as a strong individualist. Move him to an unchallenging nine-to-five job, and Jack would go bananas.

Have you ever thought about how your own mental abilities might relate to your career satisfaction and success? To some degree, it's helpful to think about our mental styles—but it's nothing to worry about. A great majority of jobs place a higher priority on such things as showing up on time for work each day than they do on extraordinary mental ability. Although intelligence obviously does have an influence on leadership potential, so does energy, drive, self-confidence, and determination. In fact, a person with average mental ability who's willing to work hard will often leave a mentally brilliant underachiever in the dust!

A long-term study of one thousand children in California who were tested and found to be gifted in intelligence showed that over a twenty-five year time span very few of them had reached the roster of famous leaders. None had attained high political office, become the CEO of a large corporation, or the president of a college. Only 5 percent were in *Who's Who*, and only 13 percent were in American Men of Science.[3]

But what about the influence of IQ on creativity? Common sense and the findings of personality researchers tell us that information processing, which is an aspect of IQ, plays a part on one's ability to think creatively.

With the most broad brush stroke, one could paint two very contrasting mental styles that have been proven to exert some influence on one's creativity. A complex thinker will understand ideas by breaking them down into their smallest units of matter, and by recognizing the relationships among them to varying degrees. A concrete thinker, on the other hand, will digest and arrange information into a less complex, more simple outline. Complex thinkers are better suited to entertaining theoretical ideas and forming elegant strategies, while concrete thinkers form a more practical, albeit one-dimensional, view. *Both styles have some general advantages and disadvantages.*

Complexity. Do you frequently entertain complex theories or abstract ideas? Do you enjoy solving various types of puzzles or unknowns? Do you have an above-average IQ? Do you frequently catch hidden meanings in thoughts and events that others miss? If so, you're a complex thinker. You seem to discern similarities and differences between ideas without difficulty.

Chances are, you figure things out by understanding the intricacies of the problems and how they relate to solutions. Your mental abilities are well developed, and you are able to pursue a variety of topics in depth, irrespective of their difficulty. Depending upon your style, you may come across to others as highly theoretical, or easily understood and practical. The complex thinker who takes into account the unifying elements of a situation will discuss things in a clear and concise manner. This is the communication style that I like to call "simple, but on-target." The other variant is the complex thinker who, impatient with what he considers as too "simplistic," keeps discussions at a theoretical, academic level. This is what I call the "See how smart I am!" variation. Because your intellectual abilities are likely to be recognized by others, you may enjoy playing the role of the expert, teacher, or helper. Make sure, however, that your co-workers don't see you as an "out of touch academic," or worse yet, as "arrogant"!

If you're a complex thinker who's not exactly a "people person," you may find that your closest friends are actually in the world of ideas. Your intellectual affinity with an author or poet from another century, for example, may seem closer to you than a real friend, co-worker, or perhaps even a loved one. To this extent, the extremely bright are sometimes alienated from people and dis-associated from the world that most others experience.

Complex thinkers are usually most comfortable in jobs that pro-vide some variety and intellectual challenge. Behavioral and biolog-ical scientists, physicists, space scientists, physicians, chemists, mathematicians, and managers in highly technical fields are just a small sample of the type of occupations that provide opportunities for complex, abstract reasoning.

Tips for Complex Thinkers

- Just because you're intelligent doesn't guarantee that you'll make practical decisions or meet deadlines. Complex thinkers often entertain new theories and techniques until their minds are cluttered with a glut of new details. Beware of "analysis paralysis." There is a time for analyzing and a time for action. When back flow happens, remember to return to the basics.

- Guard against acting like a professor in a think tank. Come off it, professor! Move beyond discussing the intricacies of the prob-lem and learn to communicate with others in a simple, clear fashion. Wanting to keep things complicated may be rooted in a low self-image.

- Keep in mind that even the best job-to-person match involves work that is mundane and routine. Make certain that you don't overlook the dull aspects of your work. It's like eating your veg-etables; they may not be as exciting as eating dessert, but no job is 100 percent fun.

- *Managers:* Make sure that intellectually gifted workers have enough challenge and variety. Whenever plausible, let them ana-lyze information and make decisions.

Concrete Thinking. Do you think on a common-sense level more than theoretically? Do you find yourself puzzled by the meaning of philosophical discussions? Do you get frustrated when people explain theories rather than talk straight? Do you prefer literal meanings over highly symbolic meanings in literature? Have you come from an educational environment where competence was not pushed?

Concrete thinkers usually see things in terms of black and white. They make decisions by looking at facts that are readily apparent. Concrete thinkers value simplicity and straightforwardness—why complicate life? This practical, common sense style lends itself toward good business decisions if matters are quite straightforward and uncomplicated. The downside, however, is that concrete thinkers may overlook "hidden" meanings or may not grasp difficult subjects as readily. This problem is intensified when a concrete thinker also has an indirect focus. In this instance, a person's mind will wander while failing to recognize important distinctions.

Linda worked in the quality department of a large manufacturing firm. She was given three months in which to compare four competing statistical process control (SPC) software packages. Then she would make recommendations to upper management as to which software package was best for a project application. Although Linda was seen as a bit absentminded, she seemed like the right person to do the analysis because of her degree in computer science. It involved learning how to use each of the software programs and then developing a real world application to see how each one performed.

Linda started her research by reading the promotional literature published by each of the software publishers but eventually learned that the descriptions only gave a cursory view of the package capability. A colleague advised her to run an actual performance test, but she had difficulty understanding how a person would actually use it in the application. As her three months whittled away to just one week, Linda became extremely frustrated. It seemed like the more she tried the less she understood. At the last minute, Linda came to Susan for help. Susan was a complex thinker who was also a service-oriented people person. Together, they got the job done.

Tips for Concrete Thinkers
• Although being aware of intricacies and other nuances may not be natural for you, many things, over time, may be learned. It may take a little longer or require more training, but it can be mastered. The more you learn about a particular subject or process, the more like second nature it will become.

- Look for the subtleties of a situation before you make a decision. Are there any hidden meanings or consequences that you have overlooked? Would you benefit from some area of training that could help you in a particular phase of your job?
- *Managers:* If you are more of a concrete thinker, make sure that you take into account the individual differences among the personalities and work styles of each of your employees. Remember that not everyone is motivated by the same type of communication, feedback, or management style. Take a "tolerance pill" and hear out a complex thinker's ideas, even if he or she seems to ramble on a bit.
- *Managers:* Work cautiously with subordinates who are concrete thinkers and seek promotion. Motivated concrete thinkers sometimes "Peter Principle" themselves up the organizational hierarchy until they get over their heads in complexity. Guard against asking a concrete thinker to undertake a complex assignment without making sure he or she is adequately prepared for the task.

SUMMARY

So, where do you stand on the creativity scale? Each of the four factors we've just discussed—focus, orientation to change, experiential style, and complexity—all of these qualities make a partial contribution to one's overall level of creative thinking.

If you have an indirect focus, prefer new ideas, are open to new experiences, and can grasp complexities, you have an edge on creative thinking.

Those with direct focus who prefer tried and true formulas, are closed to new experiences, or think on a more concrete level, may not be sought out for original ideas. These individuals may, however, be great at applying solutions once they are found and distilled to the common sense level.

8

How's Your Emotional Health at Work?

Common Problem Personalities,
Though not a Comprehensive List:
Suspicion and Mistrust, Anger and Passive-Aggressive
Sabotage, Narcissism and Low Self-Esteem, Perfectionism,
Thought Disorganization, and the Antisocial Personality.

SHORTLY BEFORE CHRISTMAS, Tom arrived at his desk early one morning to find that a colleague had already been there to extend holiday greetings. "Merry Whatever!" said the typed message on a Post-It Note. Even if the note hadn't been signed, he could have guessed its author.

All of us have worked with someone whose personality is so disagreeable we can sense it a block away. Immediately, Tom knew the note was left by his boss. She was chronically angry, somewhat antisocial, and not at all easy to get along with. Most people in the department steered a wide circle as they walked around her desk. The amazing thing was, not only was she the department head, she was also the first person most people spoke with when they called the department. Most everyone in the office wondered how she managed to keep her job when she was spitting venom most of the time.

This chapter will deal more directly with the problem of the negative personality—some might say the emotionally disordered personality—on the job. Closely related is the importance of sound emotional adjustment. Most of us are reasonably well-adjusted, susceptible to the normal ups and downs of life, but we're pretty resilient overall. All of us have particular personality strengths and weaknesses, and these have been covered in earlier chapters. My purpose here is to deal with more extreme, pervasive emotional problems that lead to chronically maladjusted personalities at work.

Have you ever had to work with someone with serious personality defects? If so, you know how quickly he or she can drain your energy. Have you yourself had difficulty attaining your own personal or career goals because of some emotional problems? In either case, consider the consequences. A person's emotional health bears heavily on both career and life satisfaction.

Several studies have been conducted to determine what percentage of the American population is considered to be emotionally healthy. In some instances, people were randomly selected from census data, while in others all the inhabitants of a particular neighborhood were interviewed. Although different studies used varying criteria of what was "normal," it is interesting to note a basic agreement of their findings. Approximately one-third of the samples were shown to have emotional difficulties that were severe enough to interfere with their day-to-day lives. Another third had some measure of emotional problems, while the final third felt free from emotional difficulties.[1]

Is this "rule of the thirds" ironclad? Not exactly. Researching "optimal" emotional health is vulnerable to the biases of the researchers, including their assumptions about truth and the nature of human beings. On the other hand, possibly 5 percent of the population are truly healthy, 10 percent are severely disturbed, and everyone else is somewhere in between. Regardless of the actual numbers, it's apparent that some people are better able to adapt to the circumstances of life than others. How, at the workplace, can you tell if someone is well adjusted? While this list is not all inclusive, it provides a few general guidelines.

1. *Productivity*—Whether it's programming a computer, conducting an orchestra, repairing a broken dishwasher, or teaching children, the ability to be productive means being able to accomplish a quality and quantity of work that is consistent with a person's ability and reasonable employer expectations.

2. *Play*—Work should be balanced by times of productivity and recreation. The healthy person is able to let go of work long enough to shift gears into play. Play means doing something just because it's fun or pleasurable. A healthy person will know when it's time to take a break from the work cycle.

3. *Relating Well*—The ability to relate to people means listening to others, giving and receiving constructive feedback, and paying attention to one's own needs and the needs of others. Well-adjusted people have a pattern of interacting with others in a constructive manner—even in periods of conflict. They also exhibit an appropriate amount of trust and respect for the other person's boundaries.

4. *Fewer Symptons*—Although we all experience a certain number of stressful experiences that make us upset, tense, anxious, or depressed, a healthy person develops fewer symptons which are usually less intense and shorter in duration than those experienced by an unhealthy person.

5. *Judgment*—Healthy persons are able to think clearly and make reasonably sound decisions. They are in touch with reality and demonstrate "common sense" by considering various alternatives and consequences before acting on impulses.

6. *Dealing with Change*—How well a person copes with life's various passages has been the topic of both ancient and modern literature. The psychologist, Erik Erikson, proposed that life is full of unique, developmental challenges across the human lifespan. Adapting to the new challenges that face us at each of life's stages can be painful as well as productive. The emotionally healthy person is able to cope reasonably well to the passages of life.

7. *Identity and Self-Concept*—Well-adjusted people will basically feel good about themselves and have a sense of who they are and where they belong in this world. They have a healthy self-image.[2]

In reading the above descriptions of a psychologically healthy person, perhaps a few problem areas in your own personality crossed your mind. Although none of us is immune to all problems, the purpose of this chapter is to discuss emotional adjustment in terms of some of the more severe disturbances.

Before getting into the specifics of some personality problems, a few general comments should be made. First, most extreme personalities—at least those that lead to problems on the job—have developed from long-standing, deeply ingrained patterns and have not arisen overnight. They are pervasive and difficult to change. Many times they are so fundamental to the outlook of the person that he or she is entirely unaware of the maladjustment. In fact, the person is usually the last one to recognize his or her problems.

Second, most personality deficits are the result of chronic problems in childhood, often relating to having grown up in a dysfunctional family. Although it may seem that the latest run-in with a co-worker is solely work-related, a more objective appraisal usually suggests otherwise. That colleague may have a long history of similar problems with other employees. Others corroborate that they often feel the same way around that person. Usually, such difficulties are the result of emotional baggage that has arisen due to chronic relational maladjustment.

Emotional maladjustment may arise from several sources: absent or negligent parents; sexual abuse as a child; unresolved trauma, such as rape or incest; more acute crises such as divorce, a recent death in the family, spiritual inadequacies, or financial collapse. In general, problem personalities are a reflection of unresolved problems with some significant people in the person's past.

Third, the workplace must accommodate a variety of people and personalities. Organizations, in pursuing a profit motive, are usually not interested in promoting emotional health. Employees or even supervisors with personality disorders are often *sought* for certain positions because, for example, they will do the work of "three people," or perhaps because they are ruthless in enforcing the rules.

Employees with substantial personal problems are unlikely to change simply because a co-worker or a boss is trying to help them. Wanting or wishing a person to change isn't enough. For lasting help, they should be encouraged to seek professional counseling since their problems are deep-rooted. At best, a problem may be made manageable at work, but it will not be eliminated entirely.

Fourth, personality disorders take many forms. There is considerable overlap among each type of problem. I will discuss here, somewhat arbitrarily, those problems which tend to be prevalent in the workplace. Although this discussion should not be considered comprehensive, I believe the following types of personalities are common ones which cause much havoc in the business world.

I am going to emphasize repeatedly two alternatives to dealing with disordered personalities at work. One approach might be termed collusion, where the most extreme attributes of the disorder are harnessed for workplace effectiveness. It's similar to the old "if you can't beat 'em, join 'em!" maxim. The other is confrontation. Instead of going along with the problem employee, this approach suggests alternatives that confront the problem, in the hope of harnessing wasted emotional energy and claiming it for workplace productivity.

Personality disorders are often accompanied by anxiety. At their core, many personality difficulties are fueled by anxiety, with tremendous emotional energy being consumed in maintaining the facets of the disordered personality. Excessive, consistent anxiety on the job often reflects underlying emotional maladjustment and may well represent deep-seated personality problems. Although not all anxious persons have problem personalities, many do.

THE SUSPICIOUS AND MISTRUSTFUL PERSON AT WORK

One summer I was consulting with an organization in Hawaii. I was brought in to conduct "focus group" interviews with employees in order to diagnose the cause of some productivity and morale problems. The staff was warm, friendly, and down-to-earth. When they said, "Aloha," they meant it.

One person I worked with, however, was difficult. It was a true "Trouble in Paradise" relationship. From the outset, she was unusually suspicious of everything I did. She often interpreted my comments to mean something quite different from what I had intended. I sensed distrust, disrespect, and even contempt. For several weeks, my work became very stressful. Such people can instill self-doubt in others very easily since they are always looking for hidden motives, explanation, and evil intentions. I couldn't wait for the weekends, so I could drive to the other side of the island to refresh my mind and body.

Traditionally, extremely suspicious people have been labeled "paranoid." In general, they expect to be harmed or exploited by other people. They are guarded and read hidden meanings into harmless remarks and events. Often they question the loyalty of those around them. They are wary of nearly everything, lest someone sneak up behind them and take advantage of them. Always guarded, they have difficulty getting along with others at work and develop barriers which prevent them from forming desirable relationships with their peers. They assume everyone is out to get them. As a result, they trust no one. They will say things like, "You can't trust Jane. Her motives are always suspect," and "It's safer to trust nobody, because then you won't get taken in." They are suspicious when others are talking at work. Surely the conversation must be something negative about them!

"I'm sure I'm going to be fired," a colleague confided to me one day. We had been working on a project for some time together, and an unavoidable problem had arisen. It meant that our project would be delayed, our earlier reports were no longer valid, and we would have to begin several aspects of the job over again.

"Why?" I asked, surprised.

"Well," my colleague said, "I saw Mr. Martin talking on the phone. I'm sure he was speaking with personnel. He had that... well, you know, that look on his face—like he was thinking about me. I think he saw me looking at him. And another thing. He gave his secretary a memo to type this morning, and she smiled at me as I walked past her desk."

My friend had soon spun an enormous tale, an airtight case

against himself, so sure was he that his firing was imminent.

Those of us who have worked with extremely suspicious people know how difficult it can be to "talk sense" with them. In addition, our motives will also be suspect if we become too involved. Before long, we will be implicated in their problems as well as the villain or hero. How can the paranoid person be helped to work more effectively on the job? What lies at the heart of the paranoid personality?

At the center of the paranoid outlook lies a deep conviction that we live in a "dog-eat-dog" world. Danger lurks on every front. The person's low self-image prevents him or her from trusting others. For the extremely suspicious employee, this translates into an assumption that everyone and everything is culpable—so it's safer to trust no one. A look into the childhood of such people usually reveals many experiences in which significant adults let them down. In short, they were "taught" not to trust people.

It takes real creativity to deal with a paranoid person at work. One approach is to help the person reframe the world, his co-workers, the boss, and projects along a trust-and-mistrust continuum. To his way of thinking, people are either completely trustworthy or they are not at all. Of course, most people and situations cannot be characterized in such black-and-white terms. The suspicious employee must be helped to see that most situations do not fit such a dichotomy.

"You know, you can never trust Peter. He's always talking about me behind my back. He's just not trustworthy."

To this type of paranoid comment, you might reply, "You can't trust Peter? Never?"

"No."

"But what about the time he helped us get that accounting project done? He really went to bat for us," you might tell him.

"Yeah, that's true."

"And what about that other time..." (With a little thought, most of us can think of many ways others have been helpful, showing how they can be trusted after all!)

"Okay, you have a point," the person finally concedes.

"So Peter is trustworthy some of the time? I don't think it's black and white. I think you're right, though. Maybe there are areas where we can't trust Peter. But, on the other hand, he's trustworthy most of the time. Let's trust him with this one."

The paranoid person needs help in seeing that people are a mixture of attributes, good and bad. However, co-workers should not delude themselves into thinking that "Band-Aid" treatment is going to change a paranoid person's deep dynamics.

ANGER AND PASSIVE-AGGRESSIVE SABOTAGE

"And don't you forget it!!"

This last phrase rang in my ears as Garth walked out of his boss' office. Now what was it Garth was not to forget? That he had messed up? That that made him a lousy employee? That the little veins in his boss' head had been flexing for the last five minutes? One thing Garth would certainly not forget: the guy was always angry, always yelling, always shouting. He was a heart attack waiting to happen.

Now to another scene:

"Joe, didn't I ask you to order those spare parts?"

"Well, I guess so...I mean, I don't remember. Frank, you have to understand how busy I've been. First I had that rush order from Atlas, then the boss asked me to accompany him to lunch, and you know what really annoys me? It's my secretary; you know how she's always tying up the phone. I guess I just forget sometimes."

Anger takes many forms. Most recognizable is the angry outburst, the tirade. Garth's boss was a master at such outbursts. People almost tiptoed around his office, his authority, and his temper. He was unpredictable; the only predictable thing about him was that sooner or later, usually sooner, he would lose his temper.

More common, but much more subtle, was the anger expressed by Joe's failure to order the spare parts. He knew he was angry at Frank. He knew it, but neither of them was willing to discuss it. Yet Joe had been passive-aggressive toward his secretary, taking it out on her to get back at his co-worker. A relatively passive action (not ordering the parts) was executed (consciously or not) in such a way that his anger toward Frank was vented. Anger usually lies at the heart of passive-aggressive behavior. The result is usually that the angry person, who usually won't even admit being angry, sabotages someone else's work.

Passive-aggressive behavior is typically characterized by a passive action that represents pent-up feelings of anger toward others. Sometimes the anger is specific, most of the time it is not, perhaps building up for weeks, months, or even years.

I remember a conversation I once had with a marketing group. It seemed that their trash containers were overflowing, the carpet was always littered with those little circles of paper made by hole punchers, and, in general, the office was in shambles. Housekeeping seemed to be keeping house somewhere else! I asked them about the housekeeping department. It turned out that housekeeping was extremely upset over an unfair series of raises that had excluded them. Also they had repeatedly approached the management for better working hours, but to no avail. Although they were working, their passive-aggressive approach was taking its toll on the entire organization! Their behavior was sabotaging the efficiency of the marketing group.

Before going further, it is important to say that everyone gets angry, or perhaps should get angry. Some people think that anger is always wrong. An effective model for dealing with anger, as found in the Bible, is when Jesus was angry as he confronted and drove out the money changers and merchants who were sinning by profiteering in the temple. He did not "pussyfoot" around in his exchanges with the Pharisees. Although Paul wrote, "In your anger do not sin" (Eph 4:26), he did not suggest that we shouldn't get angry. On the contrary, he assumed that we would.

Healthy persons will get angry occasionally. But in this chapter we are talking about the chronically angry, passive-aggressive person whose personality and emotional problems cause him or her to have ongoing difficulties on the job.

Regardless of the way it's expressed, anger is usually a cognitive response to deeper emotions. That is, instead of expressing hurt feelings, angry thoughts or hostile behavior are manifested instead. Often the angry person is aware only that he or she does not like some other person but has difficulty explaining why. When confronted, most passive-aggressive people will deny their anger. In fact, they often insist that they seldom get angry, that they have a real distaste for angry people. Only after some reflection are they able to recognize (and sometimes not even then), that they are harboring strong negative feelings toward others.

Jim was limping around the office, swearing under his breath, red in the face, shirt untucked, looking more than a little disheveled. Sally asked if he was angry.

"Angry? Angry??!!" Jim was silenced by the overwhelming experience of his own rage. Silence settled over the office, as we waited for Jim to break a substantial piece of furniture.

It is not always easy to help an angry person reflect on his or her feelings. Sally should have been awarded a Silver Cross. A more conservative response would have been to wait for the storm to pass, perhaps for ten or fifteen minutes. Instead, she stepped into the hallway and into the fray.

"Jim, you were about to blow a gasket. What's up?"

"It's that lousy copier! I only needed three copies! I should've taught it a real lesson—could've dented it, or ripped the top off, or something. I'm sick of this place!!"

"Jim, it seems there are several things upsetting you. What else is bugging you?"

After the initial experience of anger, a co-worker will often open up about long-standing workplace peeves or problems at home. Many of these will be specific gripes that have been accumulating for weeks or months. While some will probably be related to personal life, at least the work-related problems can be addressed. Suggest that your co-worker take appropriate action—talk to the other person involved, file a formal complaint, or discuss it with his or her boss.

Emotionally healthy people will get upset on the job from time to time. That's natural. While most of us can roll with the occasional angry outburst of a fellow employee, pervasive anger must be addressed. Often the angry person needs help focusing and reflecting on the cause of the anger.

While angry employees often appear highly energized and motivated, their performance is usually inconsistent. It is far more desirable to acknowledge the anger and its specific focus. Those involved must try to help each other keep to specifics of performance, work product, or the office environment. It is important to realize that emotional outbursts do not always ameliorate angry feelings. Therefore, anger for its own sake—just "to vent it"—is seldom productive at work. To channel effectively the energy bottled up in anger, it must be let out in a focused, specific way, lest a bomb erupt, causing damage in all directions. This is not to suggest that angry confrontation should be or will be emotionless. But angry feelings must be related to specific examples and grievances. Otherwise, the person's feelings of anger will not be resolved but continue to build—only to erupt at some future time.

Passive-aggressive employees, or those who express their anger in passive ways, are more difficult to handle since they don't overtly express their anger. But a broad pattern of (a) forgetfulness, (b) procrastination, (c) poor work quality, (d) lateness to meetings, (e) a tendency to lose or misplace things, and (f) an unwillingness to accept blame for missteps will usually be apparent. On the job, passive-aggressive people can be quite disruptive in day-to-day business. If housekeeping never properly cleans the office, accumulating dust and mildew will eventually cause allergies, possibly even sickness. Although they often get their way, through their covert action of controlling situations, passive-aggressive people—most of whom have problems expressing their anger—can often be confronted effectively.

Much has been made of the value of such training for the workplace, since the best antidote for job-site anger is openness. Both employees and supervisors must be helped to express their true thoughts and feelings in a regular fashion, in ways that are direct and forthright. Passive-aggressive employees often harbor negative thoughts about their workplace. After showing up for work late almost every day for two months, Duane began to realize that he had grown to dislike his job. Had he been able to express assertively his grievances as they arose, chances are his passive-aggressive behavior might never have developed, or could have been halted at the onset.

NARCISSISM AND LOW SELF-ESTEEM

Although several specific personality disorders may arise from problems related to self-esteem and self-image, perhaps none is more prevalent on the job than good old-fashioned narcissism and its cousin, low self-esteem. Both involve erroneous views of the self, and both can be quite disruptive in the workplace. Narcissism produces a hollow grandiosity and inflated sense of self-importance. The other, low self-esteem, leads to many attitudes such as self-doubt, uncertainty on the job, and sometimes, a "poor-me" syndrome. How can you tell when an employee, a boss, or a colleague suffers from one of these personality extremes? Fortunately, both are rather easy to spot.

Most people who knew him thought Bill was a nice fellow. He was just a little proud. One day I overheard him in the lunch room advising a friend how to invest his money. He talked for almost half an hour about his own investments, never asking a question about his friend's own circumstances. On another occasion, Bill offered a secretary ten unsolicited ways she could improve her performance, and even suggested that he wouldn't make a bad secretary himself! Those who knew him were aware that Bill considered himself to be an authority on nearly every job in the company. He was the self-appointed expert willing to offer free advice on any situation that arose. He had told many of us that his IQ was at least 160, that he'd be happy to consult on various problems, and that he was seldom wrong! Naturally, most people were sick of Bill!

Narcissism on the job is a mixed blessing. Some jobs require a grandiose sense of self-importance, an overriding confidence in one's quality of being, an unshakable conviction that one is always right. An analytical expert, for example, is often welcomed on the job, and can be a real benefit to productivity. But the flip side can be quite unpleasant. Narcissists have little awareness of how they are coming across to other employees. They do not understand why they, who know so much, are not sought out more often and why, after all, they do not have as many friends as others seem to have. They do not care for teamwork, are confident in their own abilities, and seldom ask for help or admit any weaknesses. They never seem to tire of making suggestions and offering advice long after others have grown quite weary of it!

"That no parking sign doesn't apply to me." Narcissists view themselves as royalty surrounded by serfs and peasants. It's not that they don't value rules, it's just that rules don't apply to them. "Others must be convinced of my superiority. I deserve special treatment, privileges, and perks." Other people exist primarily to reinforce the narcissist's personal sense of importance. The narcissist is never to blame. If subservience is neglected or thwarted, the narcissist usually becomes upset and openly displays the nonreinforcing, noncompliant person that he or she is, especially at work.

In contrast, most of us know someone who constantly seeks reassurance on the job. "I'm just not sure I can do this," Betty would say repeatedly. She would ask for guidance from co-workers, her boss, and, at times, she would even call her mother from work for reassurance. If she had been able to channel her need for reassurance into increased effort at work, she'd have been a real asset to the company.

Low self-esteem is seldom helpful on the job or any other place. Self-doubt, indecisiveness, constant people-pleasing, and unmet potential not only characterize an extreme lack of self-esteem but are reflected in the work produced. Although self-esteem is not an end in itself, it must sometimes become a focus at work when its consequences become unmanageable.

In the religious context, such people sometimes exemplify a variety of "worm theology," identifying only with their sinfulness. Yet Jesus died for all, and his life and sacrificial death reflect the worth of each person. It is paradoxical that we are both worthy and sinful at the same time. A positive tension exists between the two poles if we are to function happily in the workplace. Balance is needed. It should be noted here that a low self-esteem should not be equated with humility. In faith, you cannot be truly humble unless you have healthy feelings about yourself. Negative feelings about one's self mitigate authentic feelings of humility.

Ultimately, it is this balance that a narcissistic person and someone with low self-esteem are lacking. As noted above, narcissistic energy can sometimes be harnessed for effective job performance. More often a narcissist will need gentle help to respect the expertise and knowledge of others. He or she would benefit from attending seminars designed to teach the value of teamwork, group effort, and shared responsibility. When one's narcissistic behavior becomes extreme and the person is labeled as obnoxious, it is time for a concerned boss or a colleague to confront him or her. Although the narcissistic employee will almost always become defensive, then respond with anger and hurt, "A gentle answer turns away wrath" (Prv 15:1).

Kind words can take many forms. "Bill, I really appreciate the work you've done on the committee. You've made a good contribution. But I don't think your plan for the two of us to 'take it over' is a good idea. I enjoy the team process—it's fun being a player. And we enjoy having you on the team. Let's go for mutual respect as a group, and not short-lived admiration for individual players."

At work, the narcissist needs to realize that others are also special in some way. Such a person needs to discover that constant admiration is not necessary for life and happiness. He or she needs to know that a colleague can often be a resource, and that the other person is not necessarily in a competition.

On the other hand, those suffering from low self-esteem do not need to be given continual "pride pills." Replacing the problem with a hollow sense of specialness will not be effective. Instead, such workers should be given regular, substantive feedback about the quality of their work. An occasional interpretive remark may be helpful: "You seem to have a difficult time accepting a compliment." Such direct feedback should be given only in the context of a close, mutual, nonthreatening relationship. In general, low self-esteem must be replaced with a genuine sense of worth, accomplishment, and realization of one's contribution in the workplace. John Milton observed, "Ofttimes nothing profits more than self-esteem, grounded on just and right, well managed."

PERFECTIONISM OR THE "NEVER SATISFIED" SYNDROME

Perfectionism as an extreme personality style can be very disruptive to the workplace. With it often comes a strong need for control, responsibility, exactness, and systematization, usually at the cost of spontaneity, creativity, and freedom. Although perfectionism in some contexts might be highly desirable, it is more often quite destructive.

Most of us know people who work seventy or eighty hours per week. Their stories abound. A receptionist spends hours primping lest an incoming customer find one hair out of place. A homeowner spends so much time organizing his tools in the garage that he never has time to fix anything. A co-worker spends all night preparing for a fifteen-minute presentation the following day! Most of us can think of several examples of extreme perfectionism. One wonders what can be accomplished in seventy or eighty hours that could not be done in forty or fifty.

Perfectionists can be recognized by the things they say. "Other people are incompetent, irresponsible, and lazy," or "I must be in control," or alternatively, "I hate it when I slip up like that." About others on the job the perfectionist typically says, "You should try harder and not make so many mistakes that affect my work." Perfectionists are usually adept at listing or speaking in "shoulds," as if they were universal maxims to be followed by everyone. More than anything else, they fear failure and its consequences. Their "outside" perfectionistic actions are unconscious attempts to make them feel better on the "inside." But, of course, it does not work.

Deep in the heart of the perfectionist lies a fundamental fear of being overwhelmed, of being found to be incompetent, or unloved. To control this fear, a system of rules and methods is often developed as a means of protecting against failure. In many cases, the system assumes a life of its own, to the extent that the perfectionist repeats useless protocols and habits. For example, in keeping quality management data, a co-worker used to transfer data by hand to a fresh sheet of paper rather than continue to use one that contained crossed-off items; this task often required extra hours at work (for which she was not paid). But having accomplished the task, she would sit back and say, "Ahh, I feel so much better now."

Needless to say, perfectionists often thrive in jobs requiring careful attention to detail. They may make good accountants, engineers, computer analysts, and the like. Job tailoring is extremely important in focusing the excessive energy of the perfectionist. Again, however, perfectionism may be considered a disabling personality trait when fear of failure, generalized anxiety, and feelings of being paralyzed on the job begin to replace a more functional attention to detail. A considerable amount of workplace anxiety is generated by perfectionists who fear failure.

In helping the perfectionistic to function more effectively at work, limits must be set. If your co-worker refuses to quit before a document is perfect, it might be appropriate to say, "The boss said this should take no more than four hours. I vote with him. Let's quit after four hours and call it good enough." Or, before an employee spends too much time on a job, he or she can be transferred to another project, then given feedback on the quality of the work to date.

Perfectionists need to know that their work is acceptable long before they may deem it "perfect." Further, the perfectionist can be challenged to reconsider the "shoulds" that are so fundamental to their work habits. "Who said that Scotch Tape™ 'should always' be placed so that its edge is exactly parallel to whatever it's stuck to?" Humor can often help dispel ridiculous perfectionism. At other times, "shoulds" often take the form of derogatory judgments about others at work. These can be addressed in team meetings and in feedback sessions. In addition, the perfectionist might be challenged to compare the values and standards imposed on oneself, as compared to those of one's co-workers.

Is there an important place for perfectionists? Indeed, there is. In fact, when I see a doctor or fly on a plane, I pray that the surgeon or the pilot is a perfectionist!

TYPES OF THOUGHT DISORGANIZATION COMMON AT WORK

Thought disorders will be covered only briefly, since someone whose thoughts are truly disordered will usually have difficulty holding or keeping a job. Several types of disordered thoughts can be identified: hallucinations, delusions, loose associations, impoverished thought and speech content, as well as extreme cases of personality disorders.

Most of us have heard of the "flashbacks" and "bad trips" associated with the use of drugs such as LSD. These refer largely to hallucinations—hearing voices or seeing people that others do not see. In addition, drug users often experience visceral sensations (such as ants under the skin) that have no basis in reality. The more severe psychiatric disorders, such as schizophrenia, are often characterized by hallucinations.

Delusions are firmly held beliefs that are clearly not true. A friend of mine recently worked with a patient who was hospitalized for disorientation and possible dementia. When questioned why he was in the hospital, he explained, "I was supposed to deliver five pieces of mail for the Post Office. I got lost so they sent me here." He stuck with his story during every contact my friend had with him. He firmly believed he was hospitalized on Post Office orders.

More common than delusions and hallucinations are disorganized thinking patterns, which are most commonly experienced as loose associations or impoverished speech content. A loose association occurs when two thoughts are only loosely associated, as in, "I drove to work this morning, rather than taking the car pool. I really should have let the dog out before I went running this morning." Impoverished speech is characterized by minimal, one- or two-word responses when a longer explanation is appropriate. Impoverished speech and blunted affect (almost no variation in emotion, regardless of what is being said) are often associated with depression.

A personality disorder characterized by severe thought disorganization, on the other hand, is serious. It requires more focused psychiatric treatment. Others on the job are likely to recognize a problem, even if they are able to say nothing more than, "Sue is acting weird today, is she all right?" Over the long haul, a true thought disorder will prevent effective functioning on the job, and will generally cause severe impairment in normal activities of daily living. Someone with a real thought disorder will have difficulty dressing, shopping, getting around, and interacting with other people. Often there is a sense that such a person is "living in another world."

Most of us have encountered situations on the job, however, where we must work with someone whose thinking patterns are somewhat disrupted. There may be many reasons for this: not enough sleep, a personal emotional crisis, a drug-related reaction. A fellow employee may have suffered from a neurological disorder, such as a traumatic brain injury, a stroke, or a developmental disability. Any of these can lead to marked impairment in clarity of thinking, as well as to impaired performance at work. What can be done not only to manage some of the difficulties they face at work, but also to help them to enjoy their jobs?

Personality problems related to confusion, loose associations, inability to concentrate, impaired memory, visual-spatial deficits, ongoing hyperactivity, and the like can be addressed in a limited way at work. More important than determining the precise cause is to recognize the symptoms for what they are. Persons with these troubles need help recognizing their limits. They should be encouraged to take breaks or time off when their thought-related disorder becomes unmanageable. A recovering stroke victim should be helped to understand and work within new limits, and extra help and patience should be afforded him or her.

Many people in the work force have mild neurological impairments. Such conditions may stem from prenatal circumstances, birth trauma, genetic factors, severe illness, accidents, falls, and the like. *These co-workers may be attractive, intelligent, talented, and completely unaware of their condition.* But a supervisor or manager may notice that this particular employee may not be able to remember work he did a few days before. He may frequently skip paragraphs while typing or be unable to follow more than two or three instructions at one sitting. He may also become easily frustrated. Supervisors should be alert to such behaviors and make allowances for them. *It is important to remember that all behavior is caused by some underlying force.*

In general, those suffering from thought-related problems should usually be given concrete tasks that help them to focus their thoughts and energies. "Mary, first I would like you to call each of these people and let them know their orders have been shipped." When Mary has completed the task, she might be encouraged to do the next job, one step at a time. Complex, multi-tiered, and multi-step commands will add to the frustrations experienced by a man or woman who has a thought disorder. Extra patience, structure, and an awareness of limits not only on the part of the affected person, but also among the entire staff, will help the worker with these problems to function maximally on the job.

THE ANTISOCIAL PERSONALITY

Antisocial personalities, also known as psychopaths, can be some of the most difficult people to work with because their trademarks are deception, manipulation, illegal acts, lack of remorse, superficial charm, and lack of conscience. They pick and choose which societal rules they will adhere to and the threat of punishment rarely stops them. Extreme antisocial personalities often wind up in jail because of their treacherous deeds and impulsiveness. Ted Bundy and Charles Manson quickly come to mind in describing extreme, blatant psychopaths.

Research shows that most antisocial personalities do not get better in psychotherapy. Instead, they play head games with the psychologist and improve their vocabulary so they can beat the system! The majority of antisocial personalities, however, are not serial killers. Rather, they may be friends, relatives, or co-workers living right in your community.

On the job, you will more likely encounter borderline antisocial personalities who are of the less extreme variety. More often, these are the employees who lie on their resumes, ingratiate themselves to their bosses, seduce or blackmail people, get other people to do their work, steal inventory, manipulate their "friends," and forge documents.

"In cunning we trust" is their heartfelt motto, and they often fantasize about making easy money and committing perfect crimes—large and small. I once heard of an in-house repairman who said he was discarding major pieces of electronic equipment which were broken. In fact, he was repairing them at work and taking them home to sell. He would even suggest to various departments that this or that needed to be serviced when he only wanted to make additions to his personal electronics collection. This type of fraud is more endemic to the workplace than one would think.

Although antisocial employees who outwardly steal profit financially from their endeavors, they often get bored and will quit their jobs for a new, more exciting challenge. The exceptions, however, are the most intelligent and cunning psychopaths who, as "Dr. Jeckles and Mr. Hydes," infiltrate the system and work within it for quite some time.

> They appear to function reasonably well—as lawyers, doctors, psychiatrists, academics, mercenaries, police officers, cult leaders, military personnel, businesspeople, writers, artists, entertainers, and so forth—without breaking the law, or at least without being caught and convicted. These individuals are every bit as egocentric, callous, and manipulative as the average criminal psychopath; however, their intelligence, family background, social skills, and circumstances permit them to construct a facade of normalcy and to get what they want with relative impunity.[3]

Through deceit, superficial charm, manipulation, and exploitation of the work environment, these men and women can wreak havoc on group morale and company productivity. They have their own self-centered agenda.

Judas Iscariot provides a helpful biblical example of the antisocial personality. It is likely that throughout his association with Jesus, he was running the treasury to his own advantage. In response to others' suspicions and questions, he probably sought to maintain the appearance of innocence and feigned ignorance of any wrongdoing. Finally, he betrayed his Lord with a kiss. An act of affection conveyed the most evil of intents, betraying his antisocial personality and his cunning intentions.

What can be done to cope with the antisocial employee? Where outright crime is involved or suspected, evidence should be gathered and reports should be made through proper channels. Personal confrontation, however, should probably be avoided. Cross an antisocial personality and you're in for trouble because they often follow through on their threats to have "the last laugh."

In addition, guard against your weaknesses. Self-doubting, ambitious, or egotistical persons are seen by the antisocial person as easy marks for manipulation. Interactions with antisocial persons should be direct, work-related, and pertinent to ongoing operations. Guard against discussing your personal affairs with this type of manipulator because he or she will soon seduce you with an unsolicited solution that will be hard to resist. Soon, the person's likely to have you hooked.

In addition, guard against becoming a co-conspirator in any type of work-related manipulation and deceit. "Hey, I found these executive meal vouchers out back. What do you say we use them to go down to the club? They'll think we're Mr. McAndrew and another VP. No one will ever know. I even know where the parking spaces are."

A simple "no thanks" may anger an antisocial co-worker, but it will at least preserve the working relationship, and send strong signals that you want no part in any schemes.

SUMMARY

In this chapter we have discussed severe personality problems and the impact they have on work performance. These problems are distinguished from the personality styles described earlier, since they are often debilitating and can severely affect job performance. Although such people know that they are experiencing difficulties at work, they are often unable to put a finger on the exact nature of the problem. Usually, bosses and co-workers have already noticed and labeled such people.

Although stereotyping can be tempting, it is important not to label your co-workers. This means that, although a person may seem to fit a stereotype, he or she still deserves a fair shake. If we are always looking for problems in our co-workers, we'll find them.

We tend to find what we are looking for. But continually labeling our colleagues is an ineffective means of dealing with particular problems. *Each person is unique and worth understanding and will appreciate it when we treat him or her as such.*

Rather than labeling, it is suggested that personality-related problems be understood and dealt with as they arise. Discrete behaviors, words, and patterns should be addressed as they occur. Although it may be tempting to think, "Well that confirms it. Dr. Narramore said they would act this way." That sort of reaction will not help in addressing the root problem or the specific behaviors. It is precisely because no one is understanding and being direct with them that people with disordered personalities remain that way. No one has the courage or skills to confront them in a focused and helpful way.

Keep in mind, however, that you are not a professional therapist. Nor are you paid to give counseling sessions to fellow employees during working hours. This means that you'll probably have little opportunity to help such a colleague to change. But you can try to understand and refer the person to competent outside help. This approach will call for you to be more patient. Your job is to learn to get along with your fellow employee in spite of his or her emotional disturbances or quirks.

Once again, it is important to emphasize that personality disorders such as those described in this chapter are usually caused by a long history of problematic relationships with significant people, such as parents, siblings, and teachers. They are deeply ingrained patterns of behavior and perceptions that affect most of life. They usually require professional counseling and will seldom be completely resolved by changes at work. Extensive professional counseling may be necessary. In some cases, medication may be needed.

Managerial responses to the personality disorders should be aimed at focusing and channeling the misplaced energies of the problem person. Often this requires understanding the nature of the problem, and then developing creative responses that will maximize strengths and minimize weaknesses on the job. A paranoid person working in the customer service department of an insurance company, for example, might be shifted to a fraud investigation department. In all cases, dealing with problem employees requires a supervisor who is insightful enough to look beyond the obvious in a performance problem.

HOW IS YOUR EMOTIONAL HEALTH?

1. Do you have many unexplained cardiovascular, gastrointestinal, or respiratory complaints or frequent muscle pains?

2. Do you frequently experience thoughts or impulses that won't go away?

3. Do you frequently feel self-conscious or uncomfortable in interpersonal situations?

4. Do you frequently lack motivation, wanting to withdraw from life?

5. Do you often feel tense or nervous, or experience panic attacks?

6. Do you have persistent fears about certain things or places?

7. Do you feel isolated from people and wonder if others are out to get you or trying to control your thoughts?

8. Do you often experience feelings of guilt, or have trouble falling asleep at night?

9. Do you have frequent thoughts of death or dying?[4]

The above are *symptoms* commonly found among people with emotional difficulties. If you answer "yes" to some of these questions and feel like you are not functioning very effectively on the job, you may want to consider seeking professional help from a licensed psychologist or psychiatrist.

9

You and Your Personality: Putting It All Together

THE FIRST STEP IN APPLYING the information in this book begins by asking, "What would you like to gain from reading this book? Would you like to improve a relationship with a co-worker or your boss? In what way? Would you like to understand how to help an employee be more productive? Are you considering a new career or job? Would you like to move up in your organization? Or change something about yourself?

Whatever your motivation for reading this book, keep focused on it because that hot button will be part of what motivates you to apply the information and improve the quality of your work life. As we begin to put it all together, you're going to need a motivator to take some of the more self-directed steps that may move you out of your comfort zone. After all, its easier to ponder about personality differences than it is to apply the material. But more on that in a minute.

HOW TO DETERMINE YOUR STRONGEST PREFERENCES AND STYLES

If from the preceding chapters you've already gained a greater understanding into your own and others' personalities, congratulations! You're probably an insightful person! If the applications of this material are still a bit unclear, don't worry, the purpose of this chapter is to help you start to put it all together.

The personality snapshots which you have taken of yourself in this book are a starting place for you to begin to know yourself better. In the eight broad personality patterns in the preceding chapters, you've had a chance to look at yourself. A general pattern may have emerged or an overall style that is descriptive of you. For example, you will find yourself scoring either "high," "medium," or "low" on such general personality patterns as people orientation, extroversion, influencing others, tough-mindedness, certain types of thinking, creativity, independence, and emotional health. A high or low score would be more pronounced than a medium score, another word for a flexible score.

Putting this information to work for you involves gaining an awareness of your highest and lowest general personality patterns and then, within each of those general patterns, examining a number of *specific* subfactors related to your personality.

If you're an extrovert, for instance, do you happen to be a risk-taker as well? If you're lower on the power pattern, how would you see yourself on the specific factors of assertiveness, trust, and innovation?

Let's take a moment now to review your high and low patterns and any subfactors that seem to apply to those broader patterns. Rather than try to do too much, let's start by looking at just one or two areas that seem to be your strongest hot buttons.

Exercise One: Write down your most pronounced patterns and the subfactors which most support them. Take a piece of paper and write down the two or three general personality patterns that you see as most pronounced (this can either be a "low" or "high") in your life. Beneath each pattern, jot down a brief description of the specific subfactors which have the greatest influence on that pattern. For this exercise, you may have to scan some of the earlier chapters and jot down some notes. Or it may be enough to review the chart that I've provided on the facing page.

With each subfactor, write down what you see as your assets and strengths that are attached to it.

Next, consider the downside of those same personality factors and write down what you may need to guard against. For example,

Personality Patterns and Subfactors

Chapter One: The People Person Versus the Private Person
Subfactors:

| Play | Service | Relatedness | Dependency |

Chapter Two: Are You an Extrovert or an Introvert?
Subfactors:

| Enthusiasm | Risk | Social Participation |

Chapter Three: Of Power Plays and Power Brokers
Subfactors:

Assertiveness   Trust   Orientation to Change
Self-Concept

Chapter Four: Can We Depend on You?
Subfactors:
Rule-Keeping versus Rule-Breaking
Direct versus Indirect Focus
Concern for Order versus Laxness
Impulsiveness versus Deliberation

Chapter Five: The Way You See Reality
Subfactors:
Emotional Sensitivity
Impulsiveness versus Deliberation
Analytical Thinking

Chapter Six: Do You Fit In?
Variant Pattern: Autonomy versus Structure
Subfactors:

Dependence   Self-Concept   Assertiveness   Risk
Orientation to Change   Rule Conformity   Trust

Chapter Seven: The Creative Juices—How Your Ideas Flow
Subfactors:

Focus   Orientation to Change   Complexity
Experiential Style

Chapter Eight: How's Your Emotional Health at Work?
Common problem personalities, though not a comprehensive list:
Suspicion and Mistrust
Anger and Passive-Agressive Sabotage
Narcissism and Low Self-Esteem
Perfectionism
Thought Disorganization
Antisocial Personality

if you are high on the broad pattern of power, turn back to that chapter and review what specific subfactors have the greatest bearing on your desire to take charge of or influence other people.

If you chose the subfactor of innovation and change, you might write down that you are good at brainstorming and finding better ways of doing things. On the other hand, the downside may be that you expect others to be more openminded when actually they're not.

Exercise Two: Identify your subfactor combinations. Now that you've looked at several of your key personality patterns and underlying subfactors, go back over them and circle the three subfactors that have the strongest influence on your daily experience.

At this point look over the three subfactors which you have circled and draw a connecting line between them. Think about how these combined factors, which you have circled, could relate to your greatest likes and dislikes. Consider the aspects of your job that either energize or drain you and how these combined factors may relate to those.

Here is an example. If the three highest scores that you circled were high innovation, high assertiveness, and high risk-taking, you probably value, among other things, your independence and creative freedom. You like change and new ideas and are quite venturesome. On the other hand, you may be easily frustrated by others who limit you by not giving your ideas a try.

Exercise Three: Know yourself through understanding what you don't like. One of the approaches I use in some workshops is aimed at helping people get in touch with situations or behaviors that bother them. I conduct an exercise on behaviors or things that "really tick me off." Let's try it: make a list of ten or fifteen things people do that tend to bother you. Writing down names of people is not important. Brainstorm here. There are no right or wrong ideas. Include both large and small things that "tick you off." At first you may be hesitant to write things down, but once you get rolling you'll begin to notice that there is a pattern. Recognizing this pattern is important.

The purpose of this exercise is twofold. First, it's another way of understanding your most intense high or low preferences and personality styles. Second, it can help you recognize the situations that you would like to see handled differently. These should then be translated into statements such as, "How do you win with me and how do you lose with me?" (See pages 175-76).

The self-assessments which you have taken thus far are a starting place in terms of knowing yourself better. Now think about what you have read, and then discuss your findings with family members, trusted friends, and co-workers, so you can get some more validation and insight.

For example, you might say to someone you trust, "Carol, I've just finished Dr. Narramore's book about *Personality on the Job,* and I tend to identify with some things he mentions. I'm wondering if you would give me some honest feedback on this."

If the person gives you some fairly good feedback, that's great. But don't stop there. If you're talking with a person you trust, be even more direct about your expectation. You might say something like this: "Curtis, I need your candor. I'm not looking for compliments. I'd like to understand myself better and I'm counting on you to help me on this because this is important to me." This lets your friend know that you don't expect him to be politically correct with you—just honest. If you tell people that you expect them to be honest and frank, they'll be much more apt to do so than if you say, "If you ever notice this, just let me know."

PERSONALITY TESTS

Sometimes it's hard to see ourselves because our own self-image and its guardians—defense mechanisms—can get in the way of clear self-understanding. Like Adam and Eve who tried to hide from God in the garden, it's sometimes hard to admit the truth about ourselves. For instance, if we're too critical of ourselves, we may not be able to acknowledge certain strengths. If we're overconfident or have an exaggerated sense of adequacy, we may not be able to admit a weakness or problem.

continued on page 174

Because of the natural human bias toward self-deception, you may have answered some of the self-assessment questions in an unrealistic light.

The descriptions of the personality patterns and subfactors in this book are meant to promote insights but are only suggestive. To obtain the most realistic and complete feedback about yourself, it's best to take a professionally developed, full-length personality test from a person professionally trained in counseling, personality testing, or career development. I've summarized my views on a few of the better personality tests at the end of this book (see the appendix).

The personality discussion in this book is not meant to be as accurate as a professionally constructed personality inventory. The very best instruments available today are a result of years of exhaustive psychometric research and are copyrighted by the companies which developed them. Tests of normal personality such as the 16PF, Neo Pi, CPI, PRF, PPI, and MBTI may only be administered under the supervision of those who are especially trained in interpretation and feedback of the results.

IT'S EASIER TO CHANGE YOUR *JOB* THAN YOUR PERSONALITY

Now that you've gained some insight about your more defining personality characteristics, you're probably starting to see strengths that help you at work and weaknesses which can get you in trouble.

Would you like to change some things about yourself? Maybe that's a good idea. Perhaps not. My experience and that of many psychologists is that changing aspects of one's personality doesn't come easily. In fact, it can take years. Nor is changing oneself just for the sake of change wise. To increase the quality of your work life, the best approach is often to change the job, rather than the person.

Sue, for example, worked for an engineering consulting firm. Her particular job in the organization required that she spend most of the day by herself in a cubicle working on a computer. In terms of personality patterns, however, she was an extroverted "people person". Because Sue had learned computer skills, she was assigned to the job even though it drained her energy. A mismatch? Yes. Sue's boss, after realizing the poor job-to-person fit, moved her into a work role where she had significantly more interpersonal interaction. This matched her personality.

Don, thirty-eight, was promoted to the position of finance manager in a division of a large bank. As a rule-keeper and a traditionalist, he did well in work roles that involved dealing with numbers in a procedural, systematic way. As a private person he related to ideas more than people. As a reactor, Don found the administrative aspects of his management position to be almost overwhelming. Within six months of his new promotion, he "Peter Principaled" to the point where he was let go.

Today Don is studying to be a CPA. It's a job where his rule keeping and traditionalist side can "go by the book" without a lot of interpersonal distractions. Should Don try to change his personality so that he can relate better to people and learn to plan more realistically? If these traits are interfering with his life and he recognizes the problem and wants to change, yes. In the short term, however, moving out of management and back into a specialist's role is an effective strategy.

HELPING OTHER PEOPLE ADAPT TO YOUR NEEDS

So far we've been discussing how the quality of our job-to-person matches can be increased by making some major work changes. Without making major changes to a work role, sometimes it's possible to *modify* a job if a co-worker or boss will cooperate. To accomplish this, it's usually best to discuss this from the standpoint of, "Here's how I function best and, in turn, am best able to help you."

As we seek to understand ourselves better in relation to our co-workers and boss, we need to create a similar language so we can understand personality differences better. Then the real trick is managing those differences, because they can be powerful. Communicate your "hot buttons," for example, by helping your boss understand the benefits he or she will get by assigning you work that is within your strongest personality preferences rather than outside them. An introvert who is not very assertive, for example, should explain to a boss how a more forceful person can do a better "sell" job.

For the employee who is detail-oriented and doesn't like a lot of change or handling too many projects at once, talking to one's supervisor about how many jobs one is given at a time and then asking the boss to help set priorities will allow both worker and supervisor to perform at their optimal level. Help your boss understand that he or she will actually save time by giving you more structure because then you won't have to stop and wonder what to do or where to go next. Once the boss knows that the employee does best working on one project at a time, the work flow might be somewhat modified.

If you are an assertive, independent person, you may wish to explain to a co-worker that you react better to questions than directions. If you're a rule-keeper and you value being on time, you may wish to tell an indirect-focuser or rule-breaker about how promptness and dependabiliy affect your ability to respect a co-worker.

Remember, if we always insist that the other person change, that is not good for the relationship in the long run. The key is both asking another person to *accommodate* to your hot buttons and agreeing to accommodate to his or hers. Your co-workers have things they need from you, too.

LEARNING TO ADJUST ON THE JOB—
STARTING WITH ONE BASE HIT

Sometimes, in order to succeed on the job or get along with people better, we need to adjust ourselves. List three or four areas where you need to adjust. For example, a thinker may need to show more consideration to other people's feelings.

Bob was so task-focused and accustomed to giving orders that five of his employees had resigned. His employees dreaded going into his office because he was extremely critical. He continually put people down. One small step for Bob would be to spend thirty minutes each day with his employees without judging or criticizing any of them. Bob may not do this, however, until he sees the connection between becoming more people-oriented and the increased productivity that this would ultimately generate.

Don't start working on the aspect of your personality that is most difficult. Rather, begin with an area that will be more manageable, so you can be encouraged by your success. If you're unhappy with being introverted and you have a low self-image that you would like to change, don't expect to change everything at once. Think about what you might say to a few co-workers, for example, but don't go too far. Make a small change. Reward yourself. Then move on to another challenge. Your self-image problem may take some time to work on. Perhaps you'll need to find a friend, minister, or a professional counselor to help you. Rather than worrying about how difficult it will be to make so many big changes, just think about what you want to do differently one minute, one day at a time.

SUMMARY

At the beginning of this chapter the question was posed, "what would you like to gain from reading this book?" Achieving that goal begins by making a concerted effort to better understand your most pronounced or extreme personality patterns and subfactors. For this reason, I'd like to challenge you to *get rough with this book*. If you read about one of your personality hot buttons and can relate to a particular suggestion or tip—circle or underline it and then "dog-ear" the page. Then, do the exercises in this chapter. Later, commit yourself to discuss what you are learning with a close friend, co-worker, or perhaps a family member. That will provide you with a "reality test" and help your new insights stick.

The more you understand the strengths and weaknesses associated with your personality preferences, the more you can negotiate better work fits with others and guard against the negative consequences of your own style. So, while people persons, for example, can bring harmonious working relationships, caring, and service to any situation, they also risk being overly dependent on co-workers, avoiding tough decisions, and wasting time. Private persons, meanwhile, bring cool detachment to the job and are less distracted by interpersonal situations, but when these qualities are maximized, private persons can ignore people's feelings causing resentment and conflict.

Lastly, personality insights are no reason to excuse yourself or blame others. Be careful about labeling your co-workers or blaming your personality opposites for all your difficulites at work. Labeling others can be both unethical and dangerous. Sharing insights about a co-worker's personality should be done at the persons request and in his or her presence. When sharing insights about yourself, however, it may be advantageous to use labels if that helps a co-worker or boss understand your needs, expectations, and best work fits.

10

You and Your Boss

THERE'S AN OLD ADAGE in the corporate world that says: "Never get into a power struggle with your boss—unless you're related to the CEO."

But on the television news recently, a reporter described some recent cases where a distraught employee inversed this aphorism. One man poured gasoline on his boss and then set him on fire. One woman, disguised in a wig, "settled the score" with her supervisor by walking into his office with a loaded gun, and then shooting him.

What's going on? Were the actions of these disturbed employees extreme? Yes. Were their emotions of frustration, stress, or anger uncommon? No.

A national study conducted by a life insurance company found that one out of five Americans experiences stress because of his or her boss. Recently, I conducted an anonymous "quality of work life" study of 138 churchgoing adults from various denominations who worked for a variety of large and small companies. One of the items on the printed survey was: "Sometimes I wish my boss _____."

Thinking about *your* boss, how would *you* fill in that blank? What would *you* wish about *your* boss? This is how the 138 people in my study answered:

"Sometimes I wish my boss_____

would demonstrate better interpersonal skills."	17%
would provide better supervision."	12%
would show more respect for employees."	12%
would exhibit better work habits."	12%
would communicate better."	10%
would show Christian commitment and morals."	9%
would disappear."	7%
would deal with his or her own personal problems."	5%
other	16%

"I wish my boss...wasn't my mother" commented one employee of a family business. Another employee, perhaps representing a "Freudian slip," wrote "I wish my boss... was dead!" A deep psychoanalytic translation of this comment might read: "I hate him. I hate him. I hate him. I hate him. I hate him."

Of course, not all feelings toward bosses are negative. Some employees and their bosses get along just swimmingly. A boss who gets promoted may, for example, actually ask that a favorite employee be transferred or promoted with him. This signals a good working relationship. A smart boss will recognize the importance of keeping loyal, supportive people nearby.

I know a lady who wrote an article in which she highly praised the virtues of her boss and included it in a manuscript. But when the editor received the manuscript and read it, he refused to print it. The rejection slip read, "Not realistic! No boss is this great."

In this case, however, the editor was wrong. This woman truly appreciated the fine qualities of her boss and was being realistic.

ARE YOU STUCK WITH A DIFFICULT BOSS?

Yet as my survey indicated, many people do have bosses who give them a hard time. So if *you* are in such a situation, know that you're not alone. Perhaps you can identify with one or more of the typical laments brought to light in my survey. If so, let me ask: Do you think your boss is going to change? Does your boss have a compelling reason to make the changes you'd like to see? Is he or she even aware of certain personality hangups? Even if your boss recognizes some shortcomings, is he or she really motivated to change? Short of therapy, a major life change, spiritual conversion, pressure from his or her boss (this is risky if you're the investigator), or photographs of the boss in a compromising situation, the answer is probably no. If you have a problem with your boss, guess who feels uncomfortable? That's right—the one with less leverage.

Human personality develops early and steadily. Day by day, month by month, and year by year various influences leave their impact upon a child which now as a grown person causes him or her to act and react in a rather predictable fashion.

People can change, although they *must be aware* and convinced of the need. They must also *want to change* and the process is usually slow! Getting a boss to change is even harder because that's not part of your job description—you're not a therapist. Furthermore, if you persist, you may not have a job much longer. Rather than trying to change your boss, why not change how *you* react to your boss, which in turn, will improve the quality of your working relationship. You'll do better when you're the one who gets the insights and makes the necessary adjustments. One lady said, "My boss has a lot of problems; that's for sure. But he's as honest as the day is long. So I don't mind making adjustments that help us maintain a fairly good working relationship."

It's Not Your Fault. One of the most important principles in working with a poorly adjusted boss is this: *Don't own his or her problems.* Realize that you are not responsible for causing your boss' maladjustments. He was "that way" before you met him or her. Most of us have enough difficulties of our own without taking on someone else's. It's only natural when working closely with a troubled supervisor to identify with that person, thinking that somehow you may be involved, or may even be the cause. But as you remind yourself that you are not responsible for his or her problems, you can relax and be much happier. It naturally follows, then, that you do not have to "react" to these maladjustments. You are neither causing nor owning them. They're your boss' concerns!

Employees who struggle with a low self-image, or who are withdrawn and shy, or basically insecure, or who were mistreated as children are especially vulnerable when verbally attacked by a superior. They are inclined to blame themselves. Often they tend to feel that if they were different—smarter, better looking, thinner, perhaps their boss would like them better. In short, they begin to feel that they are the cause of their boss' bad humor.

But while they may feel that way, it isn't true. Your boss' problems developed in a unique way because of the circumstances of his or her life, but you had nothing to do with them. So ask yourself, "Am I assuming the blame for my boss' maladjustments? Am I identifying too closely with his or her hangups? Am I unconsciously accepting responsibility for the boss' problems?" This new attitude is much more objective and will help you see the situation in a more accurate perspective. By separating yourself from your boss' personality, it will enable you to be much happier at work and at home.

TIPS IN RELATING TO YOUR BOSS

Are You Listening? Have you experienced the frustration of driving through a fast food restaurant line only to receive the wrong order at the pick-up window? I must confess to have fantasized a few times about how great it would be to magically and summarily dismiss a number of fast food offenders. At most places, the server gets the order right because they have been trained to repeat the order back to the customer. That's a pretty good listening technique. It works well with nearly every one!

In the office environment, the customer is your boss because in the final analysis it's his or her directions you're being paid to follow. Not listening to a boss is one of the fastest ways to end a job or derail a career. The amazing thing, however, is that employees who don't listen well are often the last to be aware of their offensive inattentiveness. The waiting rooms of outplacement firms, for example, are filled with former employees who thought they were doing just great up until the day they were fired.

Why do some employees fail to listen to their boss? Understanding an employee's personality gives us some clues. The employee with indirect focus, for example, may be so far into deep space that he or she doesn't pick up what the boss is saying. Lax employees don't care what others think. Independent and assertive employees have their own agenda. Risk-takers may not share the boss' need to be cautious. Overly confident employees may disregard the boss because they think they know better. Insecure employees, on the other hand, may find the prospect of asking their boss for clarification to be threatening. In addition, if a boss is a feeler, he or she may have an idea, but it may not be articulated very well. If you are a thinker, you may miss some of the subtleties of his or her meaning.

For these and other reasons, it's vital to make sure you're cooking up what the boss ordered—then deliver the goods. John, for example, was asked by his boss to give a training presentation on a certain topic to the employees from a unit of his department. Although his boss had clearly indicated the content focus of the presentation, John used over half of his time talking about something else that he felt was more important. John was never given another training assignment. "He's a lone ranger," said his boss, as he shook his head.

Ask, Don't Insist. How does your boss react when you recommend a change? Does the boss resent it, ignore it, or is he or she happy for the opportunity to improve the department? Some bosses find it difficult to accept input from a subordinate—especially if their hot buttons revolve around power, independence, insecurity, or suspicion.

A boss with a desire for power or control will be predisposed to interpret conversations as competitive situations where winning is the objective. An independent boss will be on guard against anything that restricts his or her freedom or autonomous choice. While an insecure boss will be defensive in order to protect a fragile ego, a suspicious boss will mistrust your motives and either withhold information from you or require a substantial amount of information from you.

When making a suggestion to your boss, a basic rule is to put yourself in his or her place; ask yourself how you would like to be approached. Generally, this means posing what you have to say in the form of a question or adding it to one of your boss' existing ideas.

Example: Rather than telling your boss—"I think we're including entirely too much detail in our reports—no one reads them," you might ask. "Do you think we might be including too much detail in the reports? I noticed, and perhaps you did too, that the department heads don't seem to be reading them."

The second approach leaves it up to the boss to decide if he or she wants to do it the way you are suggesting. Your boss can answer yes or no. It takes the pressure off you and doesn't come across as though you, an employee, are telling your boss how to run things.

Very indirect: Perhaps your boss is a "Mr. or Ms. Control" who micromanages everything. Rather than telling him or her that you're being suffocated and to get off your back, it would probably be more avantageous to wait for a time when you're having a friendly conversation, then ask the boss about his or her preference in doing a job. "I noticed the head office gave you a lot of say-so on that project," you might say. "Do you work best when you're given more independence?" If he or she agrees, you might respond by saying, "I think I'm the same way. In fact, on the XYZ project, I'm wondering if I could have a few days with the engineering team before you meet with them to go over the specs?"

How direct should you be with your boss? The answer depends on (a) how secure the boss is, (b) how much he or she respects you, (c) the amount of directness the boss wants from employees, and (d) how much time he or she has to talk with you. If your boss likes "straight talk" and you feel secure in your job, then by all means get right to the point—in a respectful fashion, of course. But simply because you like to be direct, that doesn't mean you should always function that way.

If you're overly assertive or insistent, you may initiate a power competition. A corporate vice president of a multinational firm that I interviewed puts it this way: "Don't get into a power struggle with your boss. You may lose by winning. Making your boss angry or making him feel inferior may help you to feel good for awhile, but the consequences won't be worth it. You could lose out on a promotion or even lose your job. When it comes to a showdown, don't attempt to match wits with your boss. The person in the hot seat has the final say—otherwise, he or she wouldn't be the boss."

Understand What's at Stake for Your Boss. Your boss may not have time to explain what's going on, but he or she may be struggling with numerous pressures. At lower organizational levels, supervisors don't demand much from employees except to show up on time, do the job, and stay out of trouble. At higher levels, however, bosses will need to work much more closely with subordinates and also rely more on their help. As bosses climb the corporate ladder, they must increasingly contend with politics, competition from rivals within the organization, economic factors, personnel problems, and other concerns which weigh heavily on their minds. Perhaps it's a certain quota that must be met to keep the company out of financial trouble.

Ask yourself what stakes are involved for your boss. What's in the back of his or her mind? How is the boss looking at things? What's important to your boss? And to whom is he or she responsible? What deadlines does your boss face, and how significant are they? How can you help him or her meet them?

Learn Your Boss' Style and Expectations. To be successful at work you need to learn *what* your boss expects of you and *how* he likes you to work. Every boss has a style, a way of looking at things, a certain way of performing. Smart employees will make it a point to learn the boss' style, then adapt to it. A boss who values rule-keeping and order, for example, will want your work done promptly and accurately, and will want you to use your time efficiently. "Shoddy work" to this boss might mean disorganization or not being punctual. An independent boss may place a higher emphasis on the results you produce, not caring *how* you go about your work, only that you get it done without bothering him or her with excuses or problems.

For employees or bosses who have a lot of "hot buttons," being flexible is often difficult. If one or the other must adapt, however, it's usually the employee who must make the change.

How can a subordinate learn a boss' style and expectations? The answer is simply to observe and to ask. With a new boss, the earlier you do this, the better. To this end, a few typical approaches might be: "I'd like to be as helpful to you as possible, and I'm wondering if you could fill me in on some of your basic expectations?"

"What's important to you?"

"Do you have a game plan that I should be following?"

Once you understand how your boss works and what he or she expects of you, the chances of enjoying a successful working relationship are much higher. Your job is first to observe and learn, then deliver what he or she wants!

Of course, understanding your boss' expectations is only the beginning of an important feedback process. Periodically, it is important to check with your boss to make sure that you're producing what is needed. In some organizations this process is formalized into a *modus operandi* such as "managing by objectives." If you and your boss don't have any objectives in place, consider setting up some of your own. Periodically, meet with your boss to discuss whether you're doing what he or she wants you to do as well as *how* the boss wants it done!

Loyalty. One of the most effective ways to be loyal is never to talk behind your boss' back. No matter how tempting, don't succumb to the office gossip circle by contributing juicy tidbits about your boss. If you know things about him or her that are less than complimentary, avoid the temptation to share them with fellow workers. And should you have a gripe or a disagreement, if at all possible, discuss it between the two of you at the first opportunity. Going to a higher authority is dangerous for you to do because you don't know your boss' connections. Furthermore, it isn't forthright and aboveboard.

"It's always best if you don't stick your boss in the back," advised Brad, as he remembered the time that gossiping about his boss got him unofficially demoted to the outside circle. "I didn't think any of my co-workers would leak what I was saying—but someone did. Even though my boss hasn't said anything to me, I'm now blocked from going any further in my department."

Loyalty also includes doing things the way your boss wants them done. Be wise enough not to make comparisons, "But, Mr. _____(your former boss) did it differently!"

Who cares how your former boss did things! Unless you're asked, it's best if you don't volunteer such information. And above all, don't say, "But we've *always* done it this other way. It's never been done like this before!" Again, who cares! Your boss has a right to decide his or her own method of getting the job done. Your job is to cooperate by catering to the boss' wishes.

Why would an employee be disloyal? People with personality hang-ups are often unconcerned with loyalty; they are too taken up with their own concerns and difficulties. An insecure person, for example, may be tempted to gossip because he or she feels unimportant, and telling tales on the boss is a means of getting attention. Rule-breakers and independent persons think more in terms of being loyal to themselves. Low assertors who have a difficult time expressing their anger or frustration may be disloyal because of their passive-aggressive tendencies. In short, they are getting back at the boss for something that upset them earlier. A person who is low on trust may also find it difficult to be loyal because he or she learned early in life that other people can turn around and hurt them, or even abandon them. The suspicious person, placing very little confidence in other people—including bosses—will sometimes have the attitude, "You better get them before they get you."

In addition, for some people it may simply be a matter of never having been taught the importance of loyalty—starting with their childhood. Many boys and girls grow up without understanding the importance of loyalty. Many have never seen it demonstrated by divorced or quarrelsome parents.

Loyalty does not include violating one's own moral standards or breaking the law. If your boss is dishonest and wants you to assist

188 / Personality on the Job

in a cover-up, you will probably be right in "blowing the whistle."
Doing this, however, can put you in a very delicate position. Since
you can't be sure of your boss' connections, you could find that
you are discussing the problem with someone in a higher position
who is also involved in the wrongdoing with your boss. Even if you
should find an honest supporter at a higher level, you are going to
need hard evidence and support in the organization. Even so, you
may be branded throughout the company as a tattler. If you can't
be loyal to your boss or the organization, undoubtedly you should
look for other employment. It's not healthy to go through life
being alienated from those around you.

Oops! Your Boss Isn't Perfect. It's helpful for an employee to
realize that nearly every boss is under pressure in some way, and he
or she can make mistakes too. There's a tendency, however, for us
to expect our bosses to be almost flawless. After all, "they get the
big bucks and have all the power, so mistakes are intolerable."

But bosses are human. If they happen to offend you, be big
enough to extend some grace. Your boss might be having marital
problems, or perhaps one of the kids is in trouble. Maybe the boss'
mother is seriously ill and he or she must arrange to provide medical attention for Mom. Why not give your boss the benefit of the
doubt!

So if your boss barks at you about things that are not really that
important, if he or she is unreasonable with demands and expectations, don't take it as a personal affront. Just realize that the boss
may be having a difficult time handling (or not handling) life's
pressures. You just happen to be the one who is working near him
or her in that particular situation.

By refusing to accept personal blame for things that are *not* your
fault, you will feel better about yourself and be better able to cope.
It can also provide an opportunity for you to be more patient and
understanding with your boss.

This doesn't mean that you are going to *like* your boss' bad
moods or negative attitudes. What it does mean is that you can
refuse to take them personally because you are able to recognize
them as *his or her* problems and not yours.

Making Your Boss Look Good. An aspect of every employee's job that is often left out of the formal job description is the need to make the boss look good.

We all want to look good, to be thought of as pleasant and competent. If it lies within your honest ability, don't hesitate to work in a way that will help your boss to be perceived favorably. If your boss has problems with focus and dependability, for example, remind him or her of important meetings and prepare the necessary materials. This will not only help him or her, but will reflect positively on you.

I know an executive, for example, who spends a portion of his time in meetings away from the office. Customarily, he phones his secretary and tells her when he will be finished with a meeting and when he plans to arrive back at the office. But being an outgoing likable man, he usually gets delayed in conversation and arrives at the office an hour or so late. His secretary knows this, but she never puts him in a bad light when others in the office ask when he'll return. She usually answers, "I'm not sure just when he will arrive but I'll be happy to phone you when he does."

All too many people unconsciously think of their boss as a parent or a teacher from their childhood or some other authority figure of their youth with whom they had many negative experiences. Consequently, they think of their boss as the enemy. They have never learned to separate the authority figures of their past from their present boss. This is a common phenomenon. It may be somewhat true of all of us. But with some, although not readily recognized, this can become a serious problem with a boss or even a spouse. Psychologists' offices are filled with clients who have confused their boss or mate, for example, with their parent or someone who has abused them years before.

Take Initiative to Learn about the Company. There are some things that your supervisor or boss may not have time to tell you, but you should know anyhow. Unfortunately, all too many employees understand little about their firm beyond their daily routine. They have no comprehension of their contribution to the "big picture." If you're being paid by an organization, you have a responsibility to become part of the team. Learn its philosophy. Take the company's perspective into consideration. Read the employee's handbook and personnel policies. This will be hard for the lax, unfocused rule-breaker, or narcissist to do. I don't owe this company anything, he or she might reason. But you do get your salary from the company, don't you?

Learn where your company fits into the big picture. What, for example, are its goals? What is the history of the organization? Is there a strategy for winning over competitors? Because your boss is limited by time constraints, he or she may not be able to fill you in on the panoramic view. Without this information, however, your daily tasks may tend to become a routine and meaningless exercise. For both your supervisor and your own benefit, *you* should understand which way you're heading—and why!

Is the company experiencing financial difficulty? If so, check to see how you can help economize—even in little ways. I know a man who was an assistant to the director of Buildings and Grounds for a corporation. One evening he read an article about a substantial savings which a company might realize if it used a different type of lighting. He called the advertiser's representative and made an appointment to learn the details. He then secured the exact cost for converting the company's present system, as well as the savings over a period of one year. When he had his facts and figures together, he showed them to his supervisor. Before long they adopted the new system which after only six months was saving the company a large sum of money. Action like this contributes to both career and organizational success.

SUMMARY

Because each boss has a unique personality, he or she will also have a unique style and set of expectations. Take some time to understand the unique qualities of your boss. The approaches that proved successful with your last boss may not work in your present situation.

A good working relationship with any boss involves listening, asking rather than telling, showing initiative, learning about the company, understanding your boss's style, avoiding power confrontations, and giving your boss permission to be human and make a few mistakes. Without this, your work life will be so difficult that the two of you will wish that each other would—poof! Disappear!

An attitude of respect is also essential. So when your boss asks you to do a job a certain way, don't argue about it. In addition, be responsible. When you want to adjust your hours or make a scheduling change, explain why. Don't hesitate to go the extra mile. If a job needs to be done, do it. Don't be concerned about doing more than your share. After all, you and your boss are in this job together. Like any good marriage, give more than you feel you're getting. The end result will be worth the effort!

11

Knowing Your Company's Personality

The majority of Americans are not self-employed; they work in organizations. In a sense, each organization is a mini-government complete with its own history, heroes, and cultural norms which shape the behavior of its "citizenship."

"We've earned a good reputation; keep it that way."

"Take it easy on the boss' son."

"Always wear white shirts...starched!"

"Go through proper channels."

"Never be late for meetings."

"Always smile and be polite...even if you disagree with someone."

"You better produce or get out!"

"Do your work, then leave."

"We are ladies and gentlemen serving ladies and gentlemen."

Organizational personalities are as diverse as the styles of their founders or leaders, and the tasks which the organization accomplishes. As you pick up clues about an organization's history, top management, and preferred ways of doing business, your chances for job satisfaction and even job promotion increase. Some employees spend years complaining about their company while wondering why they have not obtained more career success. These employees would have benefited early in their employment from studying the organization and learning why it functions as it does.

It's easier to live in a country if you know the laws and customs.

How can a person come to understand an organization's culture or personality? In consultation, my colleagues and I spend considerable time diagnosing the "health" of the organizations we are serving, using such techniques as manager interviews, focus group interviews with employees, staff attitude surveys, and individual personality assessment. Although most people don't have the time or training to conduct a thorough organizational diagnosis, there are questions that any observant person can ask. The way to figure out the personality or culture of your organization is to become knowledgeable in two areas.

First, be a temporary historian and find out what has happened in the past and how it has shaped the organization's thinking. How was the company founded? By whom? How did it become successful? Who were the heroes? What have been the failures—things that happened where people felt used? How have those incidents affected the organization's priorities today?

Second, be a sociologist and ask yourself, "What does this organization consider important? Who are the highly represented people in the corporation, and why? When you walk into the building, what is your first impression? Are you given a tour or must you explore on your own? What is the attitude of the employees? What feelings did you get as you walked through the place? Have you reviewed any annual reports or seen employee newsletters? Are employees involved in decisions that affect their work? Do coworkers share humor or camaraderie? "What makes things tick around here?" is a question that can have a revealing answer.

An organization's personality is greatly influenced by such factors as size, age, or life cycle. Also of significance are the type of enterprise and the personality of the leadership—past and present.

THE PERSONALITY PROFILE
OF LARGE CORPORATIONS

Large corporations typically earn over 100 million dollars annually. Companies such as Coca-Cola, Procter & Gamble, Wal-Mart, Levi Strauss, and Rubbermaid would all be examples of large corporations with massive numbers of employees on their payroll. They are often highly structured and are inclined to have many specialized jobs that are narrowly defined. Some examples of these might include accounts payable specialists, quality control engineers, a director of safety, and regional sales representatives. Theoretically, the sum of these pieces creates a "synergistic" whole. Ironically, one department may know how to replace a light bulb, but not be able to install a light switch.

Often there are five or six layers of management between the top and the bottom levels and a range of middle managers that fit into various niches in between. Recently, however, a tendency is evolving to eliminate middle managers to cut costs and streamline operations.

A large company will generally pay better than a small company and offer a better benefit plan (unless you happen to be a founder or family member of the small company). Employees of large organizations who are low risk-takers are often attracted to the job security which a large organization offers. Ironically, because of the industrial shift toward global competition, along with other rapid changes in society, many of today's big corporations are less able to provide lifelong employment than they did twenty-five years ago. So big may not always translate into more secure. In large organizations, office politics can also be frustrating because you rarely know where you stand in the company. Half of the people who are dismissed in company cuts thought they were doing okay until the day they received their termination notices.

Due to company politics, you are not going to receive promotions, compensation, and raises based solely on your ability. Many hidden factors creep in, such as whether people like you or not. And if you don't get along with your boss, you're never going to get anywhere! Large companies also have many policies and procedures in place. Reams of standard operating procedures will mean that there is a way to do everything—and you'd better follow the correct procedures. Huge staffs of people may do nothing but fill out forms for the government. This is great if you like precision, structure, and detail. The "go by the book" type of rule-keeper who seeks order will do well in this environment.

Some of the most talented and driven innovators and leaders, however, will leave a large organization if they don't make enough progress moving toward the top. This is often due to the fact that a bureaucracy stifles their bright ideas and need for advancement. In a small company, if you have a brilliant idea, you may have a better chance to make it to the top. In contrast, large systems may attract people who enjoy specializing in a particular function, or who are accustomed to doing repetitive tasks.

In terms of interpersonal relations, in a large organization a person can often disappear into the woodwork and at the end of the day have socialized very little. Generally, you are not expected to spend time after hours unless you are part of a particularly closeknit work group.

It's often possible for an employee of a large organization to remain relatively obscure. Employees of any kind will be less conspicuous in a company of seventy-five thousand, for example, than a small business of seventy-five. Introverted, private types may have less trouble with people because they can remain inconspicuous in a large organization. While "goof-balls" and "problem people" have a better chance of not being found out in a large system, *so do top producers*. It's possible, for example, to get stuck with a boss with poor interpersonal or supervisory skills who gives subordinates a lot of grief year after year but never leaves. As the saying goes, the boss doesn't *get* heartburn—he or she *gives* it!

Large businesses also have a strong task orientation resulting from a clearly defined profit motive. There is not always a place for feelers or persons with strong service motives. Because of demanding shareholders and a board of directors, large organizations must be profitable. With this profit mandate, many large organizations push employees to make a buck, regardless of the method. There are some places in a large corporation, however, where a feeler or a high service person may fit in well. These departments might include customer relations, human resources, training, wellness programs, and guest services, to name a few.

THE PERSONALITY PROFILE OF SMALL COMPANIES

Small businesses tend to have much more latitude than large businesses. And they are not usually scrutinized as closely by the government. Employment practices and bookkeeping, for example, are simpler. Small businesses also tend to have less politics—except in family ownership matters which are more easily understood. For this reason, creative, open, and independent persons will often find small companies less confining.

A small company cannot easily afford the fat of nonproducers. Everybody has to be willing to work hard or the company goes under. The employee in a small company must be flexible, willing to do lots of things including licking stamps and sorting the mail. Mr. Haroldson, for example, is the vice president of a retail clothing business. His regular duties include buying new lines of merchandise, interviewing candidates for job positions, meeting with his salespersons, working with a small advertising agency, and making public appearances. However, he's not beyond helping to move a desk, taking the company van to the garage, and even picking up some trash in the hallway.

Small companies may also be better able to plan financially because they have a better handle on where the money is and where it's going. Smaller businesses also offer more interpersonal opportunities in that so much time is spent with so few people. These bonds are further strengthened at company picnics, potlucks, and company sports teams such as bowling and softball leagues.

Of course, if you have a boss or a co-worker who is a difficult person, poor relationships are also amplified. The television show, *Thirtysomething,* for example, highlighted the close personal relationship that two men shared at an advertising agency. Their eccentric boss, however, was a brilliant, yet cold and heartless driver who showed very few interpersonal sensitivities.

Although close working relationships may prevail, the small company has little room for the free ride. It cannot tolerate someone who avoids doing the job, and with fewer employees, there are fewer places to hide. So if you don't pull your weight, it will hurt you—unless you're a family member, in which case you may have to do something extreme before losing your job. The chances of a talented, dedicated person making his or her mark is better in a small company unless that person has an inside track to the top in a large organization.

Small companies who are in a growth mode encourage risk-taking behavior since entrepreneurs often select others like them. Rule-keepers and risk-avoiders don't usually do well in this environment unless they're in narrower, more specialized roles such as bookkeepers or those in clerical positions.

Power in small businesses tends to reside mostly with one individual. You can do a lot of things, but be careful about crossing the owner or a key manager who has a lot of clout. If you do—*sayonara*. A wise entrepreneur, however, will find talented people and listen to their input. If you have a high need for autonomy or independence, a small company in a growth mode may be your best bet because you'll have more opportunities to take risks and then get recognized for your successes.

THE PERSONALITY PROFILE OF THE FAMILY BUSINESS

At twenty-two, Ted Jr. was on top of the world. He wore expensive clothes, drove a new Corvette convertible, and made a good living as manager of one of his dad's furniture stores. Ted Jr.'s last name was known all around town and when it came to women, he could "have his pick."

"I made a lot of money back then" said Ted Jr., "but I always wondered what I did to actually deserve it. My dad thought I knew a lot more than I really did—because I was *his* son. Yet, I didn't feel secure about my own abilities. I think that's why I left the family business for a couple of years—to see if I could make it on my own."

Ted Sr., a World War II hero and founder of the family firm, was a most outstanding person. His accomplishments both during the war, and later in the corporate world, were almost legendary. In terms of personality, Ted Sr. was a highly assertive, energetic, and independent guy. His furniture business was his kingdom and he ruled it with a watchful eye and an iron hand. As a "benevolent dictator," the personality of the business was autocratic and paternal.

When son Teddy had an idea, Senior would give him the equivalent of a paternal pat on the head. Ted Sr.'s psychological boundaries overflowed onto the son so that when Ted Jr. would express self-doubts to his father, they were always discounted as "nonsense." He reasoned that Teddy, who symbolized an extension of himself, would naturally be capable, experienced, and tough.

Although Ted Jr. was frustrated by his lack of involvement in management decisions and personal identity, he felt that overall, his situation was excellent. The business was adding stores at the rate of almost one a year and the future looked immensely bright. Everywhere Ted Jr. went he was respected and recognized. And he knew deep down that Dad wanted him to take over the business some day.

Ted Sr., however, knew that "some day" would be a while because Teddy needed to mature and move beyond his drinking and "playboy" lifestyle.

One evening Ted Sr. was awakened by a call from the local sheriff who was also one of his customers. "Your son has been in a serious auto accident, sir. I think you ought to get down here right away."

Arriving at the scene, Ted Sr. looked at the Corvette wrapped around a tree and wondered how anyone could survive. Then he saw Teddy in the ambulance. In a drunken state, he had sustained only minor cuts and bruises. But Teddy's date, who did not drink, died within minutes. As Teddy went to the hospital, Ted Sr. knew he would have to take charge of the situation. In the ensuing weeks, Senior used his leverage with the city and some "hush" money to the young woman's family to keep Teddy out of jail.

With the realization that he had inadvertently killed his girlfriend and with the court suspending his driver's license for a full year, Ted Jr. knew that he had been given a wake-up call and stopped drinking entirely. In the following months and years, Ted Jr. began to concentrate on his career and personal life. For the next fifteen years, Ted Jr. was a tireless and dedicated worker in the family business, and eventually married Margo, a young lady from his church. Although Ted Sr. gave his blessing on the marriage, Margo never felt like part of the family. What she realized, of course, was that she was competing with Ted Jr.'s father for a place in her husband's life. Although Teddy. learned every aspect of the furniture business from advertising to working with lawyers, he still was unable to make many significant decisions without arguing the points with his dad.

The business consumed Ted Jr. and Margo's thoughts, even in their free time. The stress of the whole situation impacted Margo where she felt their marriage was being threatened. This prompted her to see a marriage counselor. During this time, one of their furniture outlets lost its lease and another outlet started to lose money.

Ted Jr. and his father were both concerned but had opposite solutions to the problem. "The solution is to open more outlets," said Ted Sr.

"Dad, I disagree," said Ted Jr., "Have you taken a good look at the stores lately? They're run down. We need to sell off the ones that aren't making money and totally re-do our best store so we don't lose any more income."

Margo, through therapy, realized that her father-in-law had way too much control over their lives and that as long as Ted was working with his dad, they would never really be free. About this time, the family attorney handed both Ted Sr. and Ted Jr. a book by Leon Danco about the dynamics of family business. Although Ted Sr. didn't read it, Ted Jr. did. Suddenly everything that Margo had been saying made sense. They must break free from their enmeshed family if they were ever to find their own identity and be truly happy.

Saying good-bye to his father was one of the most difficult things Ted Jr. ever did. For several weeks, Ted Jr. told everyone except his dad about his plans to move on. He felt weak and powerless like a child. Eventually, however, Ted left the firm and on his last day surrendered the master key to the business to his father. Ted Jr. and Margo, after leaving the business, sold their house and moved to another state to begin a new life. They bought a small franchise that didn't work out very well and floundered for three or four years until they finally started to make it on their own in a new business.

"It was a difficult transition period," reflected Ted Jr., "but we got back our self respect. For the first time, we learned how to live within a budget." Today Ted Jr. and Margo have a small retail store that is quite successful. Eventually, Ted Jr. wants to open a larger one. They're not millionaires and they can't buy a new sports car every two years, but they're the happiest they've ever been.

Ted Jr.'s story is typical of the struggles that go on in a family business. The family business is the place where the great melodramas of family issues and business needs often vie for attention. Far from the stereotypical Mom and Pop corner convenience store, family business represents over 90 percent of all businesses in the United States today. These include sole proprietorships, partnerships, and many large corporations.[1] Together, they employ almost half of the nation's workforce.

Partly because family businesses must perform a difficult juggling act between subjective family matters and objective business concerns, only about 30 percent of family businesses survive into a second generation of family leadership.

Problems arise when siblings are promoted to high paying jobs, even though they may lack the experience, ability, or commitment. Family conflict, if allowed to fester, can erupt into an all-out war, with the business becoming the casualty. Founders who link their self-esteem to the business often resist change and are rarely inclined to hand the baton of leadership over to the next generation of leadership. This leaves many adult children of business founders in full-blown mid-life crises as they wonder who they are and what they're doing with their lives.

Family businesses can be frustrating for the nonfamily employee because he or she must deal with the politics of nepotism. They seldom make it to the top unless, of course, they marry into the family. If you never want to go higher than vice-president, fine, but if want to get ownership equity or reach the top, you may have to forget it.

Family businesses also have their advantages. For the non-family member, life can be paternalistically pleasant. Take good care of the family members, and there may be a nice bonus in your Christmas pay check. Small family businesses, like many other types of small businesses, tend to be friendly, sociable places to work. Lunch and break times, for example, often take on a more relaxed tone than with more formal and competitive organizations. No one will fire you for playing ping-pong in the company recreation area.

For family members, there are also advantages to working in a family business. These often include rare opportunities for advancement, the joy of working with fellow family members, sharing a common language and history with co-workers, and being able to trust those with whom you work.

Because there is more information available today on how to improve a family business, more and more owners are joining associations or hiring consultants who specialize in helping family firms work through critical issues. These often include:

- Motivation and training of successors.
- Selecting family business members.
- Selecting among potential successors.
- Role of the spouses as they affect the business.
- Reducing conflict between generations.
- Managing growth.
- Developing a mission and values clarification.
- Selection and use of an outside board of directors.
- Work relationships among offspring.
- Dividing equity fairly among family members.
- Motivating nonfamily members.
- Retirement, estate planning, and providing for the older generation.
- Attracting competent nonfamily managers.[2]

Family businesses that manage these critical issues can be splendid. Those that don't can be difficult to work for. As an organizational consultant, I have found that when family businesses have problems, the first one to come forward is often the son or daughter. Incidentally, this is also the one without the power who has typically suffered through a mid-life crisis. Unless the "powers that be" experience some pain, change is unlikely.

What advice should be given to family business members?

For owners, allow your children to enter the family business out of their own free choice. Never push or smother them. The best way, incidentally, to encourage your children to enter the family business is to have fun with it yourself. They'll see your enthusiasm and will often want what you have. Children who desire to enter the family business should be selected upon the basis of ability and commitment rather than age or birth order. In addition, make sure to provide family members with top-notch training and perhaps urge them to work outside the family business for a few years in order to develop their identity and to gain outside perspective.

For the spouses of family business owners or workers, educate yourself about the dynamics of family business by reading and attending conferences. If you can, join a support group of other spouses of family business owners or employees. You are not alone!

For adult children of family business owners, you may benefit from working outside of your family business long enough to get your bearings. If you have a poor working relationship with a sibling, find a reputable therapist or family business consultant to help you improve your relationship and the business.

For nonfamily employees, realize that your work group may be led by a one-man show rather than a team. In addition, there may be a limit as to how far you can go in the firm. Consider your personality style and career objectives to see if there is a fit.

PERSONALITY AND ORGANIZATIONAL LIFE CYCLES

One of the few things I can still remember from my high school biology class was that cells have a life cycle. "All living cells will either adapt, migrate, or die," said Mr. Norris. Just as people (who are made up of cells) develop and change over their life spans, so do organizations. The personality of a small family business during the founder's years, for example, will be drastically different when "professional systems managers" run the company several generations later.

The cycle often begins with an entrepreneur who identifies a market need, dreams big, takes a chance, and "shoots from the hip." If the marketplace responds to his product or service, com-

204 / Personality on the Job

pany growth will eventually follow. This, in turn, is spurred by competition in the marketplace. With competition, the consumer realizes that he or she has a wider range of options and begins making purchase decisions based more on personal and lifestyle preferences. The Model T, for example, used to be available only in black, but now cars come in scores of colors. At the beginning stage, the founder is closely and actively involved in most areas of the business and holds the key to power in the business.

The middle stage of an organizational lifestyle involves improving old products and creating new ones in an environment of increased competitiveness. This involves the need to organize work roles and goals more carefully and to employ specialists from outside the firm. As this happens, general management systems, financial systems, information systems, human resource systems, and others are established. If the founder is still involved in the business, he or she will face a new challenge of developing educated work groups because the founder is no longer able or qualified to make a number of line decisions. In addition, he or she will have to resolve key family issues such as succession and how nonfamily employees will be rewarded. The founder's ability to delegate and to find and attract the best and brightest people to work at the company will bear heavily upon whether it will make it to the next stage of organizational development.

The mature stage involves even more competition and the need for efficiency and cost control. Top executives, four or five levels removed from the hourly employee and customer alike, will need a continuous flow of valid, reliable information by which to make decisions. Political realities within and without the organization are more pronounced and there is an even greater need for specialists of all types. At this point, a company's size makes it very difficult to adapt and change. Its "sacred cows" create environments where top people leave and start their own businesses.

A COMPANY'S TYPE OF INDUSTRY

Another factor affecting the personality of organizations, both large and small, is the nature of the product or service itself.

Whether the industry involves paper products, publishing, petroleum, pharmaceuticals, or politics—each has inherently unique characteristics that affect its personality.

The factor of openness to change which involves innovation versus tradition, for example, can be seen in the typical dichotomy between automobile manufacturing and the computer industry.

Manufacturing, for example, is often slow and conservative. Innovators with new ideas should not expect a lot of changes because "we did it that way last year and it worked all right. We got that machine in 1950 and we'll use it as long as it runs." General Motors, for example, has tended to be conservative, very slow to move, and extremely ponderous... plunk, plunk, plunk.

Computer hardware and software are at the other end of the innovation scales. "Hey, think new and let's wing it, gang!" are their buzzwords. Hewlett Packard, for example, could come out with ninety-seven new products this month and four more next week, if they needed to. They'll invent the chips if they don't have them—and they'll do it now! The entertainment industry, although traditional because it keeps trying old formulas, does have pockets of creativity and innovation. A friend who recently visited a major television studio in Burbank reported a new type of creative meeting which she observed. During a brainstorming session, for example, participants would start by painting the walls of a room the color blue. Then, as individuals thought of new ideas, they would write them on the blue wall with a white paint brush.

Service industries such as hotels, restaurants, or retail sales often require long hours with low pay. Yet they usually offer interpersonal interaction and opportunities for a few who are really driven to succeed. In these, image is important and the more orderly person with good social presentation skills will often succeed faster than his lax counterpart.

Turning to other types of organizations, health care, historically, has not been particularly progressive, but is nevertheless very profitable. Government jobs offer security but you'll have to battle bureaucracy, lack of productivity, and plenty of politics. Nonprofit organizations offer meaningful work that is service and value-centered. Interpersonal relations are friendly, and there is often a sense of fulfillment and relief to be out of the "rat race." The downside is that many nonprofit companies are struggling for money, lack professional management, and have organizational structures that keep staff members underpaid, undertrained, and uninvolved in the decision-making process.

The above examples of organizational personalities as they relate to industry types are, of course, far from comprehensive. And within any given industry it's not helpful to oversimplify since each organization within a given industry will have its own distinct personality and its own unique environmental factors. *Fortune* magazine, for example, in their yearly ranking of the Fortune 500, lists twenty-five different industry categories. Within any ranking category, you may find two companies who deliver similar products or services while approaching their tasks quite differently.

THE PERSONALITY OF THE FOUNDER OR KEY LEADERS

Organizational personality is also influenced by the unique characteristics and values of the company's founder and current top management. Because of the founder's power or vision, he or she often selects employees who think or at least act along the same lines. These employees, in turn, attract more of their kind. Within a few years, this pattern of "self-selection" can establish an organizational personality type.

For example, the employees of the International Business Machine Corporation (IBM) have traditionally promoted a competitive marketing culture patterned on the aggressive, conservative, and controlling personality of their founder, Thomas Watson, Sr. His conservatism, for example, was expressed for many years by a company dress code which required male employees to wear a blue suit, white shirt, dark tie, and black shoes. "Don't go downtown in brown" was one of the company's unwritten rules.

Marriott Hotels are still influenced by the legacy of its founder, J.W. Marriott, who worked his way from rags to riches. He stood for the principles of hard work, fairness, service, opportunity, and value. Employees at Marriott know that if they put in long hours and go the extra mile, their diligence will most likely result in opportunities for training and advancement. But you have to earn your wings. Said one Marriott general manager, "This is not a company for people who don't want to work."

Take the Organizational Personality Quiz

S = Small Organization
L = Large Organization
F = Family Business

1. ___ Employees involved in a wide latitude of projects and activities requiring the use of various skills.

2. ___ Opportunity to use or acquire in-depth knowledge applied to a specific field of expertise.

3. ___ Atmosphere structured with established boundaries, defined performance expectations, operating procedures and rules.

4. ___ Company structure maneuverable and able to quickly respond to changes.

5. ___ Politics leave you wondering where you stand.

6. ___ Opportunity for companionship and service.

7. ___ Royalty class is treated with favoritism.

8. ___ Innovation brings opportunity for advancement.

9. ___ Environment is less conspicuous for those who produce mediocre work.

10. ___ More "problem people" can be found here.

11. ___ You take more risks, but pay and benefits are often not as good.

12. ___ Greatest stability is found here.

13. ___ High mortality rate in the second generation.

14. ___ Greatest trust among co-workers.

Answers 1=S, 2=L, 3=L, 4=S, F, 5=L, 6=S, L, F, 7=F, 8=S, 9=L, 10=L, 11=F, 12=L, 13=F, 14=F

SUMMARY

Each organization has its own unique characteristics which create predictable roles for employees to follow. The closer your own hot buttons match the behavioral requirements of your company and your job, the more enjoyable your work will be.

Have you thought much about whether your present company and your job fit well with your most pronounced personality patterns and factors? If you're looking for a new job, consider whether it would be a better or worse person-to-organization match. Sometimes it is difficult to tell from the outside. The goal, nevertheless, is to examine how well your strongest personality preferences fit with the personality of an organization. If you're an extrovert, for example, does the position in question offer you enough risk, excitement, variety, or people interaction? If you have strong autonomy preferences, will you feel stifled because the job is highly regulated? If you're an innovator, is the company progressive enough to offer you a challenge?

Most recruiters, interviewers, managers, or business owners will talk a marvelous game during the "courtship" period. Much of the information you will be given during this time, however, will be pure hype. If you are looking for a new job, remember that you are interviewing them just as much as they are interviewing you. Besides the official interviews that may be arranged for you, make it a point to ask if you can meet with the person whom you will be replacing. If you are allowed this opportunity, find out *why he or she is leaving*. If you can, also talk with this person's co-workers, subordinates, and supervisors. Consider asking questions such as, "How do things get done around here?" or "What can I reasonably expect to be the most enjoyable and most frustrating parts of this job?" During the process, try to walk around—watch, listen, and "sniff." How well would your personality match the job and the company's personality?

When you get home, talk it over with your spouse or friends who know you well. Ask for their input.

12

Communication and Conflict

The ability to deal with people is as purchasable a commodity as sugar and coffee. And I pay more for that ability than for any other under the sun.   John D. Rockefeller

Is there someone where you work who's not exactly *easy* to get along with? Has that person hurt you in some way? From CEO to data entry operator, each of us depends on key communication skills and the ability to get along with others far more than we realize. Your ability to communicate well *with* others affects your advancement potential, job satisfaction, and your company's success. Unsuccessful or negative communication results in needless conflict and, if left unchecked, can be destructive to your career.

In this chapter, we'll discuss three important principles of communication: clarity, listening, and sharing power. We'll also take a look at the dynamics of conflict to see how unnecessary dissension may be avoided.

Jim was a regional representative for a small public relations firm with an office in the Pacific Northwest. His secretary, Charlene, managed the office while he was away on business. Jim's job required that he do a lot of travelling around the country, representing the organization and holding "power meetings" with VIPs. He was an interesting and engaging person to talk to, but if you were around him very long, you might begin to wonder whether he was more of a talker than he was the genuine article. The fact was, Jim's "extroversion" was only exceeded by his lack of dependability.

Day in and day out, Jim met with various clients and tried to convince them of his organization's superiority. If the truth were told, the greatest part of Jim's job was talking people *into* things. And he was very persuasive. The job was perfectly suited for someone like Jim who had high control needs. He got a lot of satisfaction knowing he was able to influence and sometimes even manipulate people. His job was fast-paced, and he relied heavily on Charlene back in the office to handle paperwork on proposals and to tie up any loose ends that he left dangling. When people met Jim he seemed friendly enough, but deep down he was really *not* a people person. His friendly demeanor was only a power play. In reality he was quite suspicious of others.

Charlene, on the other hand, was people oriented. Her favorite part of the day was chatting with people on the phone or talking to Jim whenever he was in the office. An accommodating person, Charlene did not enjoy being pushy or too forceful with people. Jim, however, often insisted that Charlene do just that. When he was out of town, he frequently asked her to call someone and twist the person's arm. It was really uncomfortable for Charlene. Jim could not see why it was so difficult for her to be more assertive. He blamed her, thinking, "She's headstrong and not very smart." Interestingly, high achievers like Jim often tend to be a bit narcissistic. With a grandiose view of themselves, it's easy for them to see a co-worker in a negative light when he or she doesn't measure up to expectations. "How could I have made it any simpler for that woman?" thought Jim.

But Charlene saw things from a different perspective. "Who does this guy think he is, getting himself into messes and then expecting me to cover for him and fix things up?" thought Charlene.

If, at this point, they had had enough insight into each other's personalities and been able to problem-solve successfully, the ensuing escalation in conflict would not have occurred. Instead, it got nasty.

Little by little, assignment by assignment, an unpleasant undercurrent began to build between Jim and Charlene. Both contributed to the growing problem because of their personality styles and lack of insight. But neither had the resources to deal with it openly.

Jim's indirect focus and tendency to break rules created an absentmindedness which resulted in making Charlene his enabler. Often when he missed an appointment or changed arrangements at the last minute, he would get Charlene to inform the people who were involved about the changes.

Charlene, a people person with strong preferences for service-relatedness, dependency, and accommodation, was low on assertiveness. She got heartburn when she had to face someone whom she knew would be unpleasant or even angry about some last minute change. To her, this was doing Jim's dirty work, and she resented it. Her low assertiveness and low self-confidence meant that Charlene had a difficult time telling Jim directly what she thought.

Jim, on the other hand, expected Charlene to be assertive and flexible like he was. In his opinion, her resistance to some of his assignments meant that she was either not very bright or just plain lazy. And if she had a problem with doing the job, why didn't she tell him?

One day Jim asked Charlene to send a fax to the head office to explain why he would be late in turning in his expense report. He also asked her to follow up that fax with a phone call. When Charlene called the office to explain that the fax was on the way and that Jim's report would be late, an accountant in the head office was furious. So Charlene bore the brunt of his anger. Charlene then sent a fax to Jim at his hotel, relaying the unpleasant reaction of the head office and enclosing a copy of the fax she had sent to them. In response, rather than talking to Charlene personally, Jim left a voice mail message on her phone, saying the fax was not well written and questioning Charlene's competence.

Jim's characterization of Charlene was rooted in part by expecting her to be similar to himself (a problem most people have). It was worsened by the fact that he was so self-centered. A narcissist like Jim doesn't like to take responsibility for problems. Those who rise to prominence often base their self-image on the belief that they do things the right way. If there is a problem, the cause of it can always be laid at someone else's doorstep. This narcissistic tendency—along with the fact that Jim was very assertive and shrewd —caused him to be exasperated with Charlene since in many ways her personality was the opposite of his. Yet, because Jim depended on Charlene and didn't want to make matters worse, he did not talk to her directly about his dissatisfaction with her performance as his assistant.

The job was giving Charlene a lot of grief, but she didn't talk to her boss about it. Why? Because she thought she could never stand up to him. In addition, she needed the job.

With such personality dynamics in a conflict, things can only get worse. For Jim and Charlene, the tip of the iceberg surfaced when Jim was away from the office on a business trip, leaving phone messages fast and furiously for Charlene to tie up loose ends. Charlene became overwhelmed with all of his assignments. She was also getting very lonely in the office by herself. And Jim's innuendoes about her doing a bad job kept getting stronger. The result? Guerrilla warfare!

In her passive-aggressive heart, she literally disliked Jim. "I hate him," was the thought going on in Charlene's mind each day. But she couldn't bring herself to verbalize it. To a person who's low on assertiveness, handling anger can be very difficult. When there's no release valve, frustration and anger can build to the point where dealing with it becomes larger than life. So she found numerous little ways to get back at Jim. She knew she could never win an argument with him. But she could sabotage or undermine him and his work, trying to get back at the company which he represented.

Thus, when Charlene was a little low on rent money, she had few reservations about "borrowing" a hundred dollars from the petty cash fund at the office. After all, for all the grief Jim put her through, it was almost her due anyway.

This account involves two people who failed to communicate. Unfortunately, their relationship eventually ended with hard feelings. In my experiences of consulting businesses on employee relations, cases like Jim and Charlene's are sometimes more the rule than the exception. In most cases had the people understood the differences in their personalities and communicated their needs and preferences, many of their interpersonal problems could have been sidestepped.

Learning to communicate well is a skill that one's personality style either helps or hinders. For some, learning to communicate well requires work. Remember, you can pay now, or you can pay later.

GOOD COMMUNICATORS ARE CLEAR AND DIRECT

A message is only as effective as it is clear. You should choose ideas and words that are as clear and direct as possible to ensure that the message received is the message you intended. Like radio or television broadcasting, start by transmitting a high quality, clear signal because *during the transmission process, a certain amount of reception is always lost.*

The former president of Bank of America, A. W. Clausen, said it well, "Perhaps the scarcest commodity among business executives is time. The young person who has learned to save time by presenting ideas clearly, concisely, and persuasively has taken a major step towards success."[1]

This type of communication is often easier for assertive persons, thinkers, problem-solvers, and direct focus persons who are more inclined to be task-oriented. For their opposites, however, speaking clearly is more challenging. Accommodators, lacking assertiveness, may send rather indirect messages in order to be polite. In a task-oriented work setting or when time is limited, accommodators must learn to speak up and get to the point. Feelers, whose inner emotions don't always translate well to the outside world, may lack a practical, tough-minded quality that business communication may require. Reactors, who may think without considering consequences, may cause confusion by discussing incomplete ideas or concepts that are out of sequence. Persons with indirect focus must learn to concentrate on the topic at hand and limit their internal associations which others may not understand.

Another personality factor that works against clear communication is lack of self-confidence. A person who feels inadequate may avoid saying what he or she really thinks in order to avoid the risk of being disliked or rejected. For protective purposes, the insecure communicator may actually speak unclearly.

Take for example:

Clichés	"The bottom line is that we will have to tighten our belts."
Double-Talk	"Let's talk some more to discuss our options."
Qualifiers	"I think that's a good idea except for..."

Just as a straight line is the shortest distance between two points, straight talk is usually the most effective way to communicate—unless you have a boss or organizational culture that is more indirect. Some nonprofit organizations, for example, are less task oriented and more touchy-feely.

Another part of clarity and directness involves synchronizing verbal and nonverbal messages. "It's impossible not to communicate with our bodies," say the experts. Our appearance, gestures, expressions, reactions, and, of course, our words all send complex messages that continually define how others see us and how they think we perceive them! Even silence, for example, can transmit a message such as, "You offended me" or "I'm listening."

The face and the body are intensely expressive. Our appearance, facial expressions, body gestures, and the clothes we wear all communicate messages about who we are and what our organization stands for. What are all these messages saying about us? A lot! In reality, what we convey and perceive through nonverbal communication is often more important than what we actually put into words.

How does nonverbal communication work? The way we exchange information involves a complex interplay of factors. Vocal intonation, timing, facial expressions, eye movements, and body posture all play a meaningful part. Each of these may confirm or obscure what we are saying with words. In general, our words deliver the facts, while our bodies and voices say what we really mean! When we do use words to describe our emotions, we often end up describing not so much how we feel, as what we think we ought to feel! Verbal apology, for example, may be accompanied by the facial contortion of suppressed rage or hostility.

When our words contradict our unspoken messages, others may begin to mistrust our words and rely more on what we do. Angela, for example, felt overworked. As an office receptionist and telephone operator, her job involved the work of two people and she barely got through each day. When her office manager introduced her to their newest tenant, she said hello, although she wrinkled her forehead as if to say: "I am overworked and I'd rather you hadn't come."

Nonverbal language instinctively goes right to the subconscious level. At the extreme, words can become a ritual and our true messages can be conveyed wholly by nonverbal means. For the introvert or the accommodator, it is often difficult to express true feelings and attitudes verbally. This nonverbal conspiracy to cover up our true feelings isolates us and our co-workers from the honest feedback that would maximize our relationships in the workplace.

While there is no exact "Dictionary of Nonverbal Communication Etiquette," a basic rule of good nonverbal communication is to be sure there is nothing that would cast doubt on your verbal message. The following are some tips:

- Sit squarely facing the person with whom you are talking. This has the valued effect of sharing power and showing respect for the other person.
- Adopting an open posture will communicate to your co-worker or boss that you are receptive to him or her. By leaving your arms unfolded, for example, the person will feel that you are open to hearing what he or she has to say.
- By leaning toward the person you convey your interest—that you are "tracking" with him or her. This demonstrates that you are enthused by the other person's contribution to the conversation.
- Maintaining eye contact with your colleagues also greatly

enhances the communication process. Be careful, though, not to stare at the person, since doing so may send a host of unintended messages. Equally important is that you not look away. Doing so is a sure-fire way to say, "I'm not interested, I'm bored with you."

- Another key is just to relax. Enjoy your time talking with your fellow worker. You can subconsciously shape the focus of the conversation by being yourself, naturally!

- Lastly, the tone of your voice can either be a "soothing balm" to your boss or co-worker or it can be an irritant—a sort of "verbal mosquito" that the other person would just as soon want to swat away! Be aware of the sound you emit! You can, through the assistance of voice lessons, change the quality of your voice.

When I think of a person who relates well to others and is an effective communicator, I think of a lady named Beth. She is well adjusted. Consequently she doesn't have to protect her self-image. She's also clear and direct. She doesn't send out mixed messages. Her words and her actions fit together. Remember, making your verbal message consistent with your nonverbal message will increase your believability.

GOOD COMMUNICATORS LISTEN

Of all the aspects of communication, listening is one of the most important, yet it is usually the most neglected skill. This is especially true in organizations where communication relies more on the spoken than the written word.

Although people assume they are good listeners, few actually are. Amazingly, most American adults only retain about 25 percent of what they hear.[2] Not listening wastes time and hurts feelings. Why do we typically forget three-fourths of what we hear?

A common barrier to listening is when we try to listen to two simultaneous conversations, both of which are competing for our attention. Another deterrent to listening can be our own preconceived notions about the message. For instance, we may assume that the message will be uninteresting or irrelevant, so we tune out what is being said. Or we often assume that what we are hearing is too elementary or beneath our level of knowledge. On the other hand, we may think that the subject is too complex or demanding for us to understand.

From a psychological perspective, a person who is suspicious or angry toward another person will have a hard time listening to the "enemy." Someone astutely said, "You can't spit and swallow at the same time." When we're angry or mistrustful toward another person, we want to "spit" out our venom and punish the offender rather than "swallow" or listen to what he or she has to say. Individuals who have subconscious or "repressed" anger may not be aware of the extent to which their anger blocks their ability to listen.

A person with a low self-concept may also have a difficult time listening. One who has unresolved difficulties will often be thinking about his or her own problems rather than hearing what others are saying. This anxiety creates a competition that is similar to trying to hear someone while simultaneously listening to a Walkman that's turned up full blast.

Another personality aspect that can block a person's ability to listen is when he or she has an unrealistically high self-concept. An over inflated sense of self is a form of narcissistic thinking which thrives on being right at the expense of others being wrong. When listening to another person, the narcissist hears just enough to confirm any doubts or suspicions about the other person.

In contrast, the creative or absentminded person may have a hard time listening because his or her focus is loose and wandering. An indirect focuser, for example, may hear a few words in a conversation, then start free associating new thoughts of his or her own which will effectively tune out the other person's words like a short wave radio with faulty reception.

Although there are many barriers to listening, most of us listen well enough to get by. This tends to make us lazy. After awhile, most of us take listening for granted, even though we tend not to do it well. The solution is to never take for granted that you understand entirely what the other person is saying. If a co-worker says, "When you have time would you look over these reports," that message is ill defined. What is meant by "look over," and when does the other person need it? Does the co-worker need it by closing time today? Or is the deadline sometime next week?

GOOD COMMUNICATORS SHARE POWER

Communication at work serves many purposes. It can be a means of accomplishing a task. It can also be a way of reaching out to help someone or a means to forming a friendship. It may be an important exchange of information. Or perhaps it's an avenue to clarifying our own ideas or releasing strong feelings. Communication can even be used in an attempt to control events and people. In summary, communication is a vital tool all of us use to meet a variety of needs.

Peers who communicate well are the ones who share power. Although each person has his or her own opinions and feelings, one doesn't "railroad" the other into accepting one's point of view. In the earlier personality chapters, we discussed the extent to which people like to exert control or power over others. Although the power differences between two people are seldom verbalized, they are germane to communication and conflict.

One of the greatest challenges for persons with strong power preferences is to learn how to communicate nondefensively. By avoiding being judgmental toward your boss or colleague, you will not give him or her the impression that you are superior. Think of how others treat you when they differ with you.

Let's look at a couple of power distributions that can adversely affect communication.

Assertive versus Assertive. As noted earlier, assertiveness is usually the measure of how much a person wants to get his or her own way rather than comply or cooperate with someone else. When co-workers are high on assertiveness, they are usually more interested in winning than understanding each other. If neither is willing to bend, they can be at each other's throats—even if it means destroying the department or even the organization.

One solution for two power players is to divide up areas of responsibility and put a little space between themselves. "You can have the say-so in that area, but this other area will be my baby." In this way, they get out of each other's hair. Both are high on wanting power, so problem-solving usually doesn't work. It comes back to the distribution of work: what responsibilities they have, and what goals they share.

High versus Low Assertiveness. If you're not careful, you'll get into a situation much like Jim and Charlene's. The quiet, non-aggressive person is not going to communicate his or her true feelings because that doesn't feel safe. So the person is likely to retreat. This doesn't mean the person inwardly accepts being a loser. It just means the one low in assertiveness will bide his or her time and come back another day! Such an employee may even ambush you—resorting to guerilla warfare. On the other hand, the person who is high on assertiveness views communication as an opportunity for a good, clean fight and can't understand why the other person withholds his or her ideas or feelings when feeling unhappy. It's very important for both persons to take the responsibility to make sure they're communicating well.

If you're extremely aggressive or dominant, you may not even realize how aggressive you are. Half of the assertiveness classes around the nation are filled with people who are already assertive! They may be there because they are unaware of their assertiveness, or have feelings of guilt, or are hostile or dissatisfied. It's important that you build some time into your daily schedule to listen to others. You will need to ask questions, seek sincere feedback, and make sure that things are okay with your boss and co-workers. They may be threatened by you and feel that it's not a level playing field. They may believe that they can't win the game, so why play it. In fact, your colleagues may not be telling you things that are important to your mutual success.

By keeping communication lines open and respecting the feelings of others, you can prevent your colleagues from resorting to underhanded passive-aggressive attacks. Not only that, but the person with low self-esteem may withhold significant information from you. There's more than one way to get back at another person in the workplace. But is that a risk you want to take?

The low-power person must be careful not to become engulfed by others. Sometimes such a person enjoys other people telling him or her when or what to do all the time. In a work situation, though, it's often not good because if one person does all the thinking and telling, the input of the other person is lost. And that input may be vital to the workplace.

Accommodator versus Accommodator. The next power combination has to do with two people who are both low on power. When it comes to managing others, they both back off. The result of this can be a "don't rock the boat" approach. Unfortunately, it can become an "avoidance" dynamic as well. When two people are low on power, one of the biggest problems is that they blend into each other's predictability. They follow certain traditions and continue doing things a certain way because they've "always done things that way." The status quo remains the constant, and they don't adjust to the changing need of technology, the marketplace, and their customers.[3]

SELF-ESTEEM AND COMMUNICATION

So often our egos are on the line. In a very real sense, the workplace is a proving ground for our self-esteem. One aspect of our self-esteem is the need to feel competent. And communicating effectively and getting along in the workplace is often considered an important measure of our competence. Those who have a very low self-image may find it difficult to accept any feelings or perceptions of failure. They may employ defense mechanisms such as blaming others (projection), denial, or rationalization.

The other end of the self-esteem spectrum relates to having such an overly confident sense of self that you tend to think you can do no wrong. When there are difficulties, you may not "own" your part but consider them all as someone else's problems. In fact, you may see any problem as someone else's fault. Once again, this relates to the narcissistic personality type. So when we talk with people at work, we're doing more than just sharing facts that relate to company business. In a real sense, we're letting people know who we are and wondering if they think we're okay. This is why the wise employer, manager, or co-worker will try to depersonalize decisions that are made at work. Nondefensive communication is very important.

It's a manager's job to evaluate subordinates, but he or she doesn't have to put them down. Through listening, asking questions, or giving the benefit of the doubt, the boss can sidestep a self-esteem land mine.

When decisions have to be made at work or when problems arise, self-esteem always kicks in. We could call this pride or ego. A common mistake people make is that in discussing something, they tend to talk about the end results rather than the problem at hand, or why there's a difference of opinion.

People many times have a vested interest in their solution, especially those with low self-esteem. If you reject their *solution*, they interpret that as a personal rejection. Tom, for example, has a low self-image. He's intelligent and competent, but deep down he does not feel good about himself. If you were to study Tom's reactions in office meetings, you would notice something interesting. His ideas are always a part of himself. When he throws an idea into the pot for discussion, he always throws himself in with it. If you criticize his ideas, he takes it as a personal affront. Is Tom aware of this? Not at all. In fact, the group hasn't figured it out either. They just think of him as being rather obstinate and derogatory.

RESISTANCE—THE TELL-TALE SIGN OF CONFLICT

When communication breaks down, conflicts usually begin through some form of resistance. It may be subtle or passive. Just because you have a personality conflict with someone doesn't mean you'll be aware of how it's affecting you. You may ask someone to do something and that person asks you for some more information. Asking for more details can be a way of resisting you. When someone floods you with details or anecdotes or puts you off, he or she may be resisting you. Resistance may also take the form of questioning the practicality of your decision or request.

When resistance comes in the form of an attack and it is straight on, you'll easily recognize it. Typically, the resistor almost pops a blood vessel and starts talking loudly in rapid-fire succession—even yelling or glaring at you. One of the ways to recognize resistance is to check your physical reactions. Is your stomach tied up in knots? Is your posture tense and defensive? If you've reached the point where you recognize some resistance, it's a tell-tale sign that there's probably some conflict at the root of it. Remain calm and try to get to the heart of the matter. It may be best to defuse the situation by giving the resistor time to cool off before you start probing to identify the exact nature of the conflict.

Of course, resistors come in other guises. Have you ever talked to someone who is confused or who feigns misunderstanding? You'd be surprised at the number of people who understand what you are saying but pretend to be confused. That's another form of resistance.

Some people intellectualize a discussion. They start talking about theoretical points. This may be resistance too. Or a person may verbally comply. A male co-worker may say he's going to do something, but he doesn't follow through.

As long as organizations are comprised of people, such forms of resistance will be inevitable. Interestingly, when conflict is handled correctly, it can actually stimulate energy and creativity. But handled incorrectly—well, you can pay now, or you can pay later.

UNDERSTANDING THE CAUSES OF CONFLICT

Think back for a minute to the last time you experienced a conflict with a co-worker. Where did it happen? Recall the surroundings. Who was present? Picture that person's posture and facial expression. Was there a blow-up? What led up to it—three months of constant complaining? What did the other person do or say that upset you? What emotion did you feel? How did you respond? What were your nonverbal cues? How did the event end? What other person in your organization has problems getting along with this individual?

You don't have to accept or like another person in order to solve a conflict. But to cope successfully, you must be aware of the other person's world. Remember the difficult person *you* were thinking of just a second ago. How do you think the other person would describe the interaction that you recalled? Would he or she see it the same way you did? Is there any motivation for that other person to change his or her behavior? What will happen if that other person does change next time? Very often when we're in conflict with another person, we focus so much on the other person's viewpoint and attitude that we fail to recognize our contribution to the conflict.

Why are you and another person having a disagreement? First, examine whether or not the two of you are communicating clearly and directly. Are you truly *listening* to each other? To what extent are the two of you willing to share power? Are you both able to understand how your self-concept affects your communication?

Beyond these factors, there are often other causes of conflict which stem from the work environment. Most of these causes relate to changes in the workplace that people find threatening and difficult to handle.

A Changing Business Climate. The complications at work are not only because certain people are unable to get along, they also happen when organizations change and go through different cycles. Organizations change as a large corporation downsizes, a small family business grows, or the economy changes. Or perhaps government regulations such as new environmental standards take effect. And, of course, technologies develop rapidly regardless of other pressures. *Change and conflict often go hand in hand.* An organization that had fifteen hundred employees recently let two hundred employees go because of lean times economically. Nothing stands still.

Competition for Limited Resources. This is when there's not enough pie to go around. On the simplest level in business, this breaks down into fear of losing something that you want. Who's going to get that promotion? Who will get to use the lion's share of the travel budget?

This is why it's so important for managers and heads of organizations to be consistent in the way they treat their employees. The less pie there is to go around, the more important it is for leadership to be fair.

In many cases, however, the perception is worse than the situation. That's why it is imperative to communicate honestly and openly, using a problem-solving method that involves all parties: management and workers at all levels. Unfortunately, if you're concerned about having to compete with others at work, you may tend not to talk about it. You may decide to dig a trench and brace yourself for battle.

On occasion as I've traveled overseas to lead tour groups, I've noticed an interesting phenomenon. People will be heading for a bank, post office, a shop, a restroom, or some other place where lines of people quickly form. As they notice each other walking in the same direction, they pick up speed, hoping they'll get ahead of several other people. Actually it becomes a race! This is an example of competition for limited resources, or at least a perception of it. We're afraid there won't be enough to go around and want our share first.

At work, even to *perceive* competition as a threat can make us perform all the harder. For example, in the organization that laid off two hundred employees, the grapevine said they were going to lay off more. You can imagine how that affected everyone's performance on the job. It's really little different from the situation where you think there's not enough pie to go around. Everyone is wondering who will be the next to go. Soon information stops flowing and people withhold important information from others intentionally. Grandstanding usually starts when people are trying to make themselves look more important.

Work Roles. Sometimes a person's job is designed to put him or her in conflict with another person. The age-old example of this is sales and manufacturing. Sales people go out and take orders. Then manufacturing or production is supposed to deliver. In a radio station where I consulted with the sales and production departments, the sales people needed commercial spots produced quickly by the production department. In fact, they usually needed them—yesterday. But the sales staff would often wait till the eleventh hour before they issued the work order. Sales would then complain that the spots produced were not very creative and had been thrown together in a sloppy fashion. Production, on the other hand, wasn't happy with sales because they usually turned in their orders the last minute. It was hard to be creative on the spot, the production people complained, particularly when you had to meet an impossible deadline. The result was that sales was not rewarded for landing new spots, while production was not rewarded for producing a good commercial. Both were doing poorly because they were not coordinating their efforts.

Here's a good example of two very different roles in the same company, in this case, departments, that conflict with each other. Some organizations need people who are innovators and others who are controllers. The controller may be the financial manager who makes an effort to limit spending money, thus curbing projects as well. By contrast, the creative type keeps coming up with new ideas. He or she is a nonstop innovator. Many employees conflict with one another because they don't see the importance of working cooperatively for the common good. So both sides tend to suffer in a dispute.

Another example of a work-role conflict is what is known as line versus prerogative. Sometimes an incompetent manager tells a subordinate to do something the manager knows little about. The subordinate knows much more, but he or she has to take orders from someone who is not nearly as knowledgeable. This can be both frustrating and counterproductive as far as the subordinate is concerned especially when the manager even refuses to acknowledge the subordinate's superior knowledge.

Work roles may also be understood in terms of levels of specialization. Someone who is high on detail, precision, order, follow-through, correctness, and role keeping will see things differently from one who is low on detail, high on variety, likes to do lots of things but not in great detail, and in general is slower on follow-through. We're getting back to expectations—they'll differ markedly in this case of contrasting roles.

TECHNIQUES FOR RESOLVING CONFLICTS

To resolve a conflict requires that you take responsibility for your part of the relationship. For some people that's difficult.

If you're an introvert or low risk-taker, you might imagine the worst that could happen if you discussed your dissatisfaction with a co-worker. Here it can be helpful to realize that *many times the worst things are not as bad as struggling with a difficult relationship day after day.*

If you're a power player or have trouble with your self-image (either over- or under-confident), it may be difficult to work things out with other people because you want your way or tend to see problems as solely the fault of others. The way to get along well with colleagues, however, is not always to win for winning's sake. Back down a little. You don't always have to be right.

There are really three basic approaches in resolving conflicts with another person: collaboration, competitive power tactics, and avoidance.

Collaboration. The first approach emphasizes resolving a problem together in a spirit of *cooperation*. The classic technique for this is problem-solving, which centers around helping parties *separate* their personal positions from the real issues. This is accomplished by concentrating on the *needs* of the parties and the organization rather than on personal preferences, rank, or the force of one's personality. Problem-solving works best when it's done in an attitude of *mutual gain*.

A classic problem-solving illustration is that of prison officials who were attending an off-site retreat in order to plan and discuss some specifics about building a new facility. Half of the workers were security personnel, and the other half were social workers or counselors. In the middle of the meeting, the topic came up about what kind of uniforms they should wear. The security people wanted full uniforms for all prison employees. The social workers wanted name tags but no uniforms. Pretty soon the conversation focused on the end product rather than the reason why each party wanted them. And persons from both departments started to dig trenches and hold to their positions.

As the two sides started arguing about the uniforms they should wear, someone said, "Let's take a vote. All in favor of the full uniform raise your hand. All in favor of partial uniforms with just name tags, raise your hand."

It happened that there were slightly more people at the meeting from the Security Department, so they won and the majority ruled.

This solved the problem, right? Wrong. What really happened was that the side which lost had such strong feelings about the matter that the discussion became quite personal. For the rest of the meeting, they became less and less involved in the discussion. They looked out the windows, made jokes, and tapped their pencils on the meeting table.

Finally, someone in the meeting got up and said, "Look, folks, I notice that we're not getting anywhere. I'm wondering if maybe one of the reasons is that we have not come to a decision on the uniform issue that everyone can live with."

Everyone agreed to talk about it some more. There was a consultant in the group, and he utilized a classic problem-solving technique. It was a way to get past the egos and self-esteem of the people involved.

He asked the group to think for a few minutes about the problem they wanted to solve rather than the outcome and the results they wanted. What was the objective? The security people said they wanted uniforms that would create respect for their position and give them a high profile, so they could be distinguished easily. The people from the Social Work Department said they wanted only the badge because they valued creating less of a barrier between themselves and the inmates. They felt the uniform would be a barrier in forming good relationships because it symbolized power.

This fruitful discussion enabled the entire group to identify the problem and pinpoint their objectives—rather than focusing on an impossible solution.

The person in charge asked them to spend a few minutes talking about the possible solutions to the problem. "Instead of evaluating each other's suggestions, let's just list any possibilities we might share in common." Before they knew it, both sides had come up with a number of possible solutions. This brainstorming helped them to develop ideas without evaluating them, their logic, or their usefulness.

The person in charge then asked group members to narrow their ideas down to the top three that they could live with, and the top one they could not live with. Finally, everyone agreed on a solution: the personnel who were in security positions would wear the full uniform complete with cap, epaulets, gun, and handcuffs on their belts. The employees who were in social work would wear a name tag only. This is something both sides could live with. So problem-solving saved the day. *You can't always resolve problems, but you can do it more often than you think with collaborative, non-defensive brainstorming.*

People with a personality pattern that is lower in creativity or innovation and higher in structure find it harder to do this because they don't want to say things that don't make sense. But that's what brainstorming is all about. If you are more of a structured type who doesn't find this easy, you can learn if you are aware of the dynamics involved.

An important aspect of such successful problem solving is empathy. Empathy is putting yourself in someone else's shoes—understanding the other person's point of view. If you're low on empathy and high on being judgmental, it's going to be hard for you to see a situation through the other person's eyes. The challenge is for you to stretch yourself and try to understand the opposite point of view. If you tend to be more tough-minded, you can repeat back to the other person what you think you heard him or her say.

If you jump to conclusions, one way in which you can improve getting along with someone else is (1) to be sure you've heard what the other person is trying to say before you react to it.

Otherwise, you may have missed the point. (2) Also try counting to ten before you react. You may be thinking in black and white, while the other person is visualizing in color.

Competitive Power Tactics. This approach utilizes *power* and emphasizes *winning, losing, and competition.* The techniques for this are coercion, office politics, and distributive bargaining. Here the relationship is usually adversarial because one side gets something at the expense of the other. A classic example is the United Auto Workers versus General Motors. Antithetical to teamwork, this form of conflict resolution tends to encourage deception, competition, or the withholding of information.

On a personal level, if you're dealing with someone who has deep-seated problems or very poor boundaries, you may need to resort to such tactics. In other words, you will have to draw a line in the sand and make it crystal clear what behavior is unacceptable. If someone has an emotional maladjustment on the job, similar to those we discussed in chapter eight, such an approach may help them avoid getting into serious trouble.

Avoidance. This approach emphasizes *avoiding* or smoothing over differences but never really dealing with them. If conflict between two warring parties is extremely intense, sometimes a cooling off period is helpful. In fact, a third party may be necessary to resolve the conflict.

However, at some point, it's usually more satisfactory for co-workers to tackle a problem before it grows and festers. Regardless of which approach you use, be sure to discuss issues fully with the disputant, so you can arrive at an agreement that is, at least, acceptable to all concerned.

THE FEEDBACK PROCESS:
A PROBLEM-SOLVING METHOD

The feedback process begins by briefly sharing your *observation* of the other person's resistance or simply stating the nature of the problem. Remember the example of the consultant who was working with the employees of the correctional facility. Things weren't progressing well, and the leader was alert enough to stop the conversation and make an observation: "Ever since we decided on the uniforms, we've ceased to be productive as a group."

Sometimes stopping the conversation and pointing out that there seems to be a problem is the wisest move. Then state it as you see it. Don't blame anyone. Just state your observation. Talk about the problem in terms of the *type of behavior* that is an obstacle to your working together. Never use sentences like, "*You* upset me." Relate your comments to a behavior. Say, "Our arguing upsets me." Keep "you" out of the conversation. Focus on behavior and actions. Never attack other people. Watch your nonverbal cues as well.

The next step is briefly to state the original *goal* of your working relationship. Do this in a way that puts the other person in a good light and gives him or her the benefit of the doubt. Resist the urge to criticize. Rather, look for and state a common denominator or reason for your work. Technically it's called the superordinate goal. You can nearly always find something in common with the person with whom you are in conflict at work. Here you might say, "John, I know that you have this company's best interest at heart just as I do."

Keep this list of helpful points in mind as we continue to consider this problem-solving method.

1. Listen and pick up the cues of resistance which can either be direct or indirect.
2. Stop the conversation and briefly make an observation of what you see.
3. Ask for any reservations the person might have.
4. Briefly state a common goal and give the other person the benefit of the doubt.
5. Ask for the other person's help directly. Ask for an agreement.
6. Shift the responsibility back to the other person.
7. Be silent and listen.[4]

Stopping the conversation with an individual does not mean sweeping the problem under the rug. Rather, you are giving yourself and the other person the space needed to confront it. Of course, your statement needs to be based on *observation* and should never be a personal attack. Here are examples: "I notice that over the last three meetings you've come in late." Or, "I notice that when I asked for your work order lately, it wasn't filled out." Or, "I was wondering if there's a problem we need to discuss?"

Now briefly state your original goal and then give the other person the benefit of the doubt. (See number four on the previous page.)

At this point, the other person may deny that there's a problem or he or she may agree. Your move is to shift the responsibility back to the other person by asking for help directly: "John, I know we both want this project to go forward, but I'd like to see if we can agree on several points. Would you be willing to do such and such?"

After you've asked for the other person's cooperation, the tendency may be to keep talking, but this is seldom wise. Instead, just listen! Sometimes the best thing you can do is to pause and wait. It may make the other person uncomfortable. It may make you uncomfortable. That's okay. Wait until he or she responds. Doing this gives both of you an advantage.

A COPING PLAN

If you have an extremely difficult person with whom you can't resolve differences, or perhaps a more powerful co-worker or a boss, your best solution may be to come up with a coping plan.

One of the first points is to describe in detail the behavior of the person whom you find difficult. Write down your understanding of why the person probably behaves the way he or she does. Have there been some instances when it was a little easier to get along with that person? Why was that? Were there some instances that were more difficult? Why? What specifically did you do or say? What type of stress management or social support do you have which will help you cope?

SUMMARY

The most important keys to communication are speaking clearly, listening well, and sharing power. When you don't say what you mean you suffer the consequences. Your time, money, and even your credibility at work may be at stake. Having an open and honest approach with co-workers and not harboring a hidden agenda will also give you added credibility when you communicate. Without clarity and directness, your colleagues may feel that you are either manipulative or not "together."

Co-workers who listen to each other create a feeling of respect and avoid the problem of jumping to conclusions that were never intended and may be incorrect anyway. Sharing power creates an atmosphere where co-workers can collaborate rather than compete. That's a win-win situation!

Epilogue

Living God's Way

I'LL NEVER FORGET THE FIRST TIME I attempted to windsurf but got stuck in the algae instead. It was at Lake Lopez near beautiful San Luis Obispo, California. Although I had taken no lessons or read instructions of any kind, I confidently launched a thirteen-foot rental board into the shallows of the lake and began to grab the wishbone-like boom in order to steer its seventeen-foot high mast and sail. Twenty-five falls later, the wind had blown the board into a cove of the most disgusting green algae I had ever seen. For the balance of the afternoon, I kept muscling my way back onto the board. Yet every time I hoisted the rig and grabbed the boom, I fell back into the slimy green algae. It was a fiasco.

In looking back on what went wrong, I realized that I had lacked solid instruction and guidance. I had relied on my natural instincts and failed miserably. For example, I had held the rig the wrong way, placed my feet in the wrong position, and often tried to sail into the wind rather than with the wind at my back. At the time, everything I did seemed intuitively correct, but it was wrong. In reality, successful windsurfing requires various hand, foot, back, board, and sail positions that, at first, seem highly counter-intuitive.

Likewise, dealing with our own personalities requires thinking and acting in ways that are sometimes counter to our natural inclinations. This is especially true when we are under pressure.

Consider these personality patterns. Extroverts, when under pressure, may try to talk their way out of situations to the point where they find themselves whipped up into a frenzy. Introverts, on the other hand, tend to clam up.[1] Assertive and independent types can become quite insistent under pressure rather than listening to the other person's point of view. Whereas, persons low in assertiveness often give in unless they're pushed too far; then they tend to explode. When under pressure, thinkers can become overly focused on problems and increasingly impersonal rather than showing warmth and emotion. By contrast, creative, lax persons may dream away problems rather than dealing with the real issues at hand. These, of course, are just a few examples of how our strengths, in excess, can become weaknesses.

So what can you do to develop a truly successful approach to life and work, especially when you're experiencing a lot of stress? The key is to turn to God's instruction manual on human nature—the Bible. The Scriptures say, for example, to have faith in God rather than relying on your own abilities, instincts, and desires. The Book of Proverbs says, "Trust in the Lord with all your heart and lean not unto your own understanding. In all your ways acknowledge him and he will direct your paths" (3:5-6).

The biblical challenge is clear: relinquish control over your natural desires and tendencies, and do as God instructs. If you are a low risk-taker, that might mean asking God to help you face uncertainty without feeling anxiety over the outcome. If you are a chronic rule-breaker, it could well mean seeking forgiveness and restitution in an area of wrongdoing or deciding to change a work habit which is dishonest. Or if you an independent and assertive person, it may involve guarding against a rebellious and arrogant nature or re-examining your plans to make sure they really fit God's leading.

The Bible calls this spiritual process of relinquishing control over your own comfort zones, walking in the Spirit. For instance, the Bible instructs, "Not by might nor by power, but by my spirit, says the Lord..." (Zech 4:6). We need to sail with the wind at our backs rather than sailing into the wind—to use an image from windsurfing.

How do you walk in the Spirit? God's Spirit is a gift to each person who asks God for forgiveness of his or her sins and professes faith in his Son, Jesus Christ. By accepting God's gracious invitation, you experience a new birth into God's family and are equipped with a new spiritual nature. If you have never put your faith in Jesus, I invite you to read the Gospel of John in the New Testament. Chapter three tells you how to find peace with God.

As you walk in the Spirit, ask God in what ways he would have you change. As a believer in Christ, you have the capacity to change right inside you—regardless of your personality patterns, subfactors, or predispositions. This is why David could pray: "Search me, O God, and know my heart; try me and know my anxious thoughts; and see if there be any hurtful way in me, and lead me in the everlasting way" (Ps 139:23-24).

How do you know if you are walking in the Spirit? The proof, as the old adage goes, is in the pudding. The Bible says that Christians should exhibit the fruit of the Spirit in their daily lives: "The fruit of the Spirit is love, joy, peace, long-suffering, gentleness, goodness, faith, meekness, self-control: against such there is no law" (Gal 5:22).

The fruit of the Spirit, then, is God's measuring stick to help you compare your behavior with his will for your life. Major growth in the fruit of the Spirit comes from praying, studying God's Word, and obeying it.

In this light, as you think of your personality "hot buttons," ask God to help you use your strengths in a way that will honor his will and advance his kingdom. Ask for the Holy Spirit's counsel when you are under pressure and find that these strengths, in excess, have become weaknesses. Seeking God's providence and direction is the biblical prescription for true happiness in every area of life and every place of endeavor—including on the job.

Appendix

Personality Testing

A VALID AND RELIABLE personality inventory or test can offer tremendous insight to individuals seeking personal or career guidance. It can reveal important and comprehensive information about one's personality in a short period of time. Through such a test, a person may well discover aspects of his or her personality that are beyond the scope of self-awareness. Likewise, a well-constructed test can help a therapist in understanding the personality dynamics of a new client. Such tests can also assist companies in making effective human resource decisions such as employee selection and training.

Although there are many helpful personality tests in use today, it's important to remember that the map created by such a test does not always accurately represent the human territory it purports to measure. This may be true for a number of reasons. For example, some personality inventories are susceptible to motivational distortion and faking. Others tend to reduce the complexity of human behavior and personality to only a few general factors. Still others reveal their test results in a very negative manner. In addition, personality instruments can be rendered out of date by rapid changes in the use of language. A personality test that was written and normed in the 1970s, for example, may use words, expressions, or references that are dated and obscure by the 1990s. All of these are good reasons for exercising care in evaluating the results of any given personality test.

Most personality inventories can be categorized into two major types: normal or clinical. Tests of normal personality seek to identify and measure individual trait differences among persons of fair to good emotional health. These would include instruments such as the Personality Research Form (PRF), the Sixteen Personality Factor Questionnaire (16PF), the Neo Pi-R, and the Myers-Briggs—to name some of the more prominent inventories.

Clinical tests, on the other hand, are designed to look for more serious problems that people may experience such as pyschosis or depression. These inventories are also called tests of abnormal personality. Some of the more well-known instruments include the Minnesota Multiphasic Personality Inventory (MMPI) and the Clinical Analysis Questionnaire (CAQ).

Obviously, the thrust of this book has been identifying a variety of normal personality traits as they relate to the workplace, although in chapter eight we considered some common emotional maladjustments on the job as well.

However, even in considering tests that measure normal personality traits, caution is in order. After all, a discussion of any psychological test to the lay person is a bit like weighing the pros and cons of various prescription drugs with someone who does not have the benefit of medical or pharmaceutical training. Therefore, the use and interpretation of personality tests are best left to those who are skillful in not only administering such tests but also in knowing how to use the results constructively. Unfortunately, there are those who claim to be experts on personality or temperament who have little psychological training or, worse still, little insight into human personality. For this reason, the lay person must carefully evaluate the claims of both the test and test giver—usually with some reputable professional assistance. Here are a few thoughts on some of the more prominent tests of normal personality.

Personality instruments vary from test to test in terms of the characteristics and the number of personality traits they measure.

The Myers-Briggs, for example, measures four personality types based on a Jungian concept of personality. The 16PF measures sixteen personality factors, while the Neo Pi-R measures thirty personality facets. The 16PF and Neo Pi-R inventories are the results of complex factor-analytic research—a more scientific way of observing, describing, and rating personality differences.

As you may have guessed, there is an ongoing controversy among personality psychologists regarding the number of personality traits and factors and how many of those factors should be tested at any given time. In a 1988 scholarly study, two researchers, Richard Gorsuch and Bryan Mershon, found that a personality system measuring sixteen personality factors was twice as accurate in predicting real life behavior as a system using only six factors.[1]

These results concur with my own observations: namely, a personality inventory with more factors usually produces increased understanding and precision; a test with less factors usually results in diminished understanding and greater generalization. Does this mean you should avoid using an instrument like the Myers-Briggs Type Indicator since it only analyses four factors? The answer is that it all depends. Rather basic tests like the Myers-Briggs have been *successfully* used in a variety of work settings, especially for team-building retreats and training sessions where time is limited. The purpose is usually to give participants a very basic handle on how they and their co-workers think and act.

For those who seek testing for career planning, psychological counseling, or employee selection I would recommend more sophisticated instruments. The 16PF, for example, examines sixteen distinct personality factors and offers the job counselor or therapist a wide range of occupational, social, and clinical data about various personality factors and combinations of patterns. However, tests like the 16PF and the Neo Pi-R are much more psychological in nature and, therefore, require a trained professional to sort through and explain the findings.

Another test worth highlighting is the Personal Preference

Inventory (PPI), published by Compass Learning Systems. The PPI focuses on a number of personal and career motivators rather than personality factors. The feedback that the test produces is less threatening and negative than standard personality instruments. Rather than examining an individual's personality at an in-depth level, the PPI is more of a communication starter that helps individuals explore what they like and dislike in light of their present job expectations.

I've just given you a flavor of a few tests that are available today. Even as this book is published, newer instruments are probably being devised. So please don't assume this short list is up-to-date or comprehensive. Besides, if you are dealing with a competent professional, you should not have to worry since he or she will be familiar with the best tests, which are not always the latest ones.

Where, then, can you go to take a top-notch personality test? Many universities and religious institutions offer testing services to the community for both career and personal counseling. In addition, a large number of psychologists, psychiatrists, and marriage and family counselors offer personality testing to their clients. In my own consulting practice, I have found personality inventories most helpful as I work with individuals seeking vocational guidance or companies needing to improve their employee selection, training, and outplacement services.

Notes

INTRODUCTION

1. "Workers Stretched to the Limits," *USA Today,* September 8, 1992, 1.
2. James Dobson, *The Strong Willed Child* (Wheaton, Ill.: Tyndale House, 1978), 19.
3. Carl Jung, *Psychological Types* (New York: Harcourt & Brace, 1970).
4. Raymond Cattell and Maurice Tatsuoka, *Handbook for the Sixteen Personality Factor Questionnaire* (16PF) (Champaign, Ill.: Institute for Personality and Ability Testing, Inc., 1970).
5. Paul Costa, Jr. and Robert R. McCrae, *Neo Pi-R Professional Manual* (Odessa, Fla.: Psychological Assessment Resources, 1992).
6. Douglas Jackson, ed., *Personality Research Form Manual* (Port Huron, Mich.: Research Psychology Press, 1984).
7. F. Thomas Dortsch, "Job-Person Match," *Personnel Journal,* June 1989, Vol. 68, no. 6, 48-61.

FOUR
Can We Depend on You?

1. "An Inside Job," *The Wall Street Journal,* February 5, 1970, 1.

FIVE
The Way You See Reality

1. Jung, *Psychological Types,* from the "Introduction."
2. "America's Toughest Bosses," *Fortune Magazine,* October 18, 1993, 40-41.
3. Raymond Cattell, *Personality and Mood by Questionnaire* (San Francisco, Calif.: Jossey-Bass, 1973).

SIX
Do You Fit In?

1. Robert W. Service, *Songs of a Sourdough.*

SEVEN
The Creative Juices—How Your Ideas Flow

1. Personal and confidential telephone interview with a former executive in the Disney organization, Summer, 1993.
2. Douglas Bray, Richard Campbell, and Donal Grant, *Formative Years in Business* (New York: Wiley, 1974).
3. David Johnson and Frank Johnson, *Joining Together: Group Theory and Group Skills* (Englewood Cliffs, N. J.: Prentice-Hall, Inc., 1987), 42.

EIGHT
How's Your Emotional Health at Work?

1. Jerry Lewis, *How's Your Family?* (New York: Brummer/Marel, 1989), 98.
2. Lewis, *How's Your Family?*, 99-101.
3. Robert D. Hare, *Without Conscience, The Disturbing World of the Psychopaths Among Us* (New York: Simon and Schuster/Pocket Books, 1993), 115.
4. Leonard Derogatis, *The Brief Symptom Inventory (BSI)*, 2nd ed. (Baltimore, Md.: Clinical Psychometric Research, Inc., 1992).

ELEVEN
Knowing Your Company's Personality

1. John Ward, *Keeping the Family Business Healthy* (San Francisco, Calif.: Jossey-Bass Publishers, 1987).
2. Ward, *Keeping the Family Business Healthy*, 138.

TWELVE
Communication and Conflict

1. David Acker, *Skill in Communication* (Fort Belvoir, Va.: Department of Research and Information, Defense Systems Management College, 1990), iii.
2. Acker, *Skill in Communication*, 57.
3. Lewis, *How's Your Family?*, 98.
4. Peter Block, *Flawless Consulting* (San Diego, Calif.: University Associates, 1981), 208.

EPILOGUE

1. Otto Kroeger and Janet Thuesen, *Type Talk at Work* (New York: Delacorte Press, 1992).

APPENDIX

1. Bryan Mershon and Richard Gorsuch, *Journal of Personality and Social Psychology*, "Number of Factors in the Personality Sphere: Does Increase in Factors Increase Predictability of Real-Life Criteria?" Vol. 35, no. 4, 1988, 675-80.

About the Narramore Group

The Narramore Group is a psychological and management consulting firm located in Pasadena, California. It provides consultation and training in organizational development, team building, change management, employee selection, focus group market research, and individual career planning.

Dr. Kevin Narramore holds a Ph.D. in organizational psychology from the California School of Professional Psychology. He is a popular speaker at conferences and seminars throughout America.

For more information, write or call:

The Narramore Group
115 Sequoia Dr.
Pasadena, CA 91105
(213) 256-6162